Jesus Against the Rapture

Books by Robert Jewett
Published by The Westminster Press

Jesus Against the Rapture:
Seven Unexpected Prophecies

The Captain America Complex:
The Dilemma of Zealous Nationalism

Jesus Against the Rapture

Seven Unexpected Prophecies

Robert Jewett

The Westminster Press
Philadelphia

Scripture quotations from the Revised Standard Version of the Bible are copyrighted 1946, 1952, © 1971, 1973 by the Division of Christian Education of the National Council of the Churches of Christ in the U.S.A., and are used by permission.

First edition

Published by The Westminster Press ®
Philadelphia, Pennsylvania

PRINTED IN THE UNITED STATES OF AMERICA

9 8 7 6 5 4 3 2 1

Library of Congress Cataloging in Publication Data

Jewett, Robert.
   Jesus against the rapture.

   Bibliography: p.
   1. Jesus Christ—Teachings. 2. Eschatology—
Biblical teaching. 3. Millennialism—Controversial
literature. 4. Millennialism—Biblical teaching.
5. Rapture (Christian eschatology)—Biblical teaching.
I. Title.
BS2417.E7J48   236'.3   78–31759
ISBN 0–664–24253–7

Contents

Acknowledgments

Permission to quote from copyrighted works has been granted by the following publishers:

Farrar, Straus & Giroux, Inc., for excerpts from the following works. From *Everything That Rises Must Converge,* by Flannery O'Connor, copyright © 1961, 1964, 1965 by The Estate of Mary Flannery O'Connor; and from *Lancelot,* by Walker Percy, copyright © 1977 by Walker Percy.

Harcourt Brace Jovanovich, Inc., for excerpts from "A Good Man Is Hard to Find," from *A Good Man Is Hard to Find and Other Stories,* by Flannery O'Connor, © copyright 1953, 1954, 1955 by Flannery O'Connor.

Alfred A. Knopf, Inc., for excerpts from *Falconer,* by John Cheever, copyright © 1975, 1977 by John Cheever. All rights reserved under International and Pan-American Copyright Conventions.

Simon & Schuster, a Division of Gulf & Western Corporation, for excerpts from *The Chosen,* by Chaim Potok, copyright © 1967 by Chaim Potok.

Viking Penguin Inc., for excerpts from *Henderson the Rain King,* by Saul Bellow, copyright © Saul Bellow, 1958. All rights reserved.

Introduction

Several years ago I received an elaborate but puzzling invitation to attend a conference in Jerusalem. It referred to a thousand Christians gathering to discuss the fulfillment of Biblical prophecy. The odd thing about it was that Prime Minister Begin had agreed to address the conference. Why would an Israeli chief executive take time to address a gathering of evangelicals? How could it serve the quest for a settlement in the Middle East, a cause which would later result in two Nobel Prizes? It didn't seem to make much sense. So I tossed the invitation in the circular file.

Then an issue of *Newsweek* arrived to throw light on the matter. Kenneth Woodward and Rachel Mark reported on the "Christians for Israel" movement. Full-page ads had been placed in *The New York Times, The Washington Post,* and other important regional papers in support of Israel's position in the Middle East. One of these, sponsored by Carl McIntire, denounced the Palestinians as "descendants of Esau . . . claiming Jacob's Land." The campaign and the Jerusalem conference aimed at convincing President Carter to abandon his evenhanded support of Arab and Israeli claims. The sponsors want the government to stop pressuring Israel to give up territories conquered in recent wars.

Part of the oddity of this heavily bankrolled campaign is that many of the sponsors have been markedly apolitical in the past. Some of these writers and preachers have bitterly denounced liberals for becoming involved in foreign policy questions. Why were the fundamentalist critics of "social activism" suddenly taking an interest in the complex issues of a Middle East settlement?

Woodward and Mark explain the motivation as follows: "In fact, the people behind the ad campaign are Biblical fundamentalists who believe that the security of Israel is necessary to fulfill Scriptural prophecies that Christ will return to convert Israel and condemn the unrighteous." In other words the sponsors are not interested in a permanent peace settlement in the ordinary sense of the term. They want Israel to regain its ancient borders so that the end of the world will come more quickly. As apocalypticists, they yearn for a final conflagration that will destroy both Israel and the Arab world, along with the majority of humankind, after the true believers are withdrawn from history in the Rapture.

A number of widely selling religious books advocate this view. John Wesley White, the Canadian theologian who works with the Billy Graham campaigns, published a book in 1977 entitled *WW III: Signs of the Impending Battle of Armageddon.* He states flatly: "The Scriptures teach that the Middle East conflict cannot be settled, and will not be settled, until Jesus Christ comes again" (pp. 164f.). White is a millennialist, which means he expects Christ to usher in a thousand-year kingdom of peace after the final warfare is ignited in Israel.

Hal Lindsey's books, which have sold more than twelve million copies in the past few years, advocate this view. His recent effort, *The Terminal Generation,* insists: "The reborn State of Israel was central to the development of world events which are predicted to lead to the last and greatest war of all time. . . . Israel is rapidly fitting into its final role. Zechariah predicted that all nations would be drawn into the final great war which begins with a dispute between the Arabs and Israel over Jerusalem." (P. 51.)

One of the sponsors of the ad campaign, *Christianity Today*'s editor Kenneth Kantzer, confirms this rather bizarre motivation in no uncertain terms, according to Woodward and Mark. "We believe that the return of the Jews to their homeland, and the reconstruction of the kingdom of Israel, are signs of the climax of earthly history—the ringing in of the millennial, perfect world." Can it really be true that leading evangelicals are supporting Israel for ulterior motives? Do they have less interest in the justice of Arab or Israeli claims than in the use of the conflict to bring the end of the world? Are they supporting an expansionist, aggressive Israeli policy because it is the surest route to World War III, the atomic holocaust that will bring life on this planet to a halt?

One of the best-kept secrets about the historical Jesus is that he would not have approved of the ad campaign at all. His attitude toward the end of the world, pieced together by scholars over the past century, was that apocalyptic warfare should be avoided rather than advocated. He opposed the end-of-time fanatics who were promoting a climactic war with Rome by citing the same Old Testament prophecies we are hearing today. When asked for the "signs of the times" that Lindsey and White have described so extensively, Jesus replied, "No sign shall be given . . . except the sign of Jonah" (Matt. 16:4). Jonah, you may recall, had yearned for the destruction of Nineveh, but divine compassion averted it. The sign of Jonah is evidence of God's will that the wicked world may be spared from the burning some people are sure it deserves.

In place of the apocalyptic schemes favored by ancient and modern fanatics, Jesus advocated a commonsense approach to history. In Matt. 16:1–3 he refers to the regularity of weather as a clue to the signs of the times, and the only regularity visible in his era was the monotonous collapse of apocalyptic schemes after they had brought disaster to those who believed. In his eloquent word to the women of Jerusalem, who followed weeping as he bore a Zealot's cross to Golgotha, Jesus warned about the consequences "for yourselves and for your children" if their men followed the course of apocalyptic zeal into the final war against Rome (Luke 23:28–31).

In contrast to current religionists who clamor for the annihilation of civilization, Jesus wept over the city of Jerusalem and said, "Would that even today you knew the things that make for peace!" (Luke 19:41–42). By refusing his message, the first-century millennialists would propel their country into a fatal war, destroying their city and the lives of thousands of innocent victims. Jesus' preference was to protect the helpless citizens of the wicked city: "How often would I have gathered your children together as a hen gathers her brood under her wings, and you would not!" (Matt. 23:37.) So it was that less than a generation after he spoke, the war advocated by the apocalypticists occurred (A.D. 66–70), with appalling loss of life and no discernible fulfillment of the Old Testament prophecies.

I call these prophecies of Jesus "unexpected" because they contradict what many Christians are taught to believe. Although the details have been understood by scholars for some time now, the strange coherence of Jesus' end-time sayings and their bearing on current issues add up to a kind of unintentional secret. The scholarly discussion is too complex for most people to follow and the current relevance is too troublesome for most scholars to bother with. The result is that sincere believers continue to be led to reject the essential message of the Lord they profess to serve. Unaware of the realistic components in Jesus' message, they fall prey to the kind of prophecies about the end of the world that have repeatedly brought disaster in the past.

To bring these prophecies of Jesus to bear most directly on the current religious scene, I compare them with the widely popular writings that comprise what might be called "the New Apocalypticism." This theology combines the dispensational perspective of the Scofield Reference Bible with a conviction that the end of the world will occur in the second half of the twentieth century. Writings of this type have come virtually to dominate the Christian Book Stores across the country. I have visited stores where more than a third of the new titles are like *The Late Great Planet Earth, The Terminal Generation, God's Plan for the Future, The Vision, You Can*

Know the Future, Armageddon, and *What on Earth's Going to Happen?*

A basic assumption of the New Apocalypticism is that the reestablishment of Israel in 1948 marks the beginning of the end times. The idea of a forty-year period of fulfillment marked by the rapture, the tribulation, and the second coming of Christ gives these speculations an urgency that appeals to concerned Christians. As Leon J. Wood states the consensus in *The Bible & Future Events:* "The clearest sign of Christ's return is the modern state of Israel. . . . One should realize that God's time-table could call for Israel to be in the land for many years before bringing the fruition of the age. But with the nation actually there, and with many factors concerning it fitting into conditions set forth in Scripture for the last days . . . one may safely believe that Christ's coming is not far in the future." (Pp. 18, 22.) Hal Lindsey has been even more specific, placing the 1980's as a kind of apocalyptic deadline.

What these books seem to overlook is that Jesus lived in a similar forty-year period, reaching from the days of John the Baptist to the opening of the Jewish-Roman War. But he used every argument in his power to dissuade his fellow countrymen from following the apocalyptic logic into the maelstrom. His gospel did not promote death and destruction, but reconciliation and life. I rather wish now that I had not discarded that invitation. It would have been right to go to Jerusalem and urge those who believe in Jesus not to make him weep yet again for his imperiled and beloved city.

The next best thing to speaking the message in Jerusalem was to put it in writing. My burden consists of seven prophecies of Jesus that throw an unexpected light on our current moment. In each case I have started by asking what the oracle would have meant for Jesus' own time. A number of recent discoveries by scholars around the world make it possible for us to understand these sayings more clearly than at any time since they were first uttered. It turns out that these authentic prophecies of Jesus differed as radically from first-century Judaism as from most of subsequent Christianity.

Though their wording is familiar, their meaning remains unexpected right down to the present moment, challenging everyone to rethink what Jesus intended his followers to believe and do.

In order to bring these remarkable poetic sayings into closer relation with modern thought, I illustrate them with relevant selections from modern fiction. The realism and penetration of these oracles are closely bound up with their imagery, so that one is driven to writers of great imaginative power to find commensurate parallels. Although Biblical exegesis does not ordinarily use materials from Saul Bellow, Flannery O'Connor, John Cheever, Chaim Potok, or Walker Percy, I have come to the conclusion that their insights are closer to the perspective of these particular prophecies than most of the traditional expositors.

When seen with the clarity produced by recent research, these seven sayings are as unsettling to modern liberals as to conservatives, as perplexing to Protestants as to Orthodox and Catholic believers. They also have a surprising relevance for current secularists who frequently agree with fundamentalists on only two points—that the end of a familiar era is rapidly approaching, and that there is little any of us can do to stop it. I am convinced that if we would get Jesus' message straight, we would conclude that the future is still open and that there is a great deal we can do. This might have an important impact on the future of the movement Jesus started and of the planet he came to save.

Chapter I

Only
the Abba
Knows

Mark 13:32–33

The most shocking and unexpected thing Jesus ever said about the end times is reported in the so-called "Little Apocalypse" of Mark. "But of that day or that hour no one knows, not even the angels in heaven, nor the Son, but only the Father" (Mark 13:32). That even Jesus did not know when the end would occur countered everything that first-century Jews would have expected of the Messiah. That the angels in heaven did not know the schedule contradicted everything that the apocalyptic tradition—including the later book of Revelation—assumed about heavenly powers opening and revealing the contents of the seals of the future. The contrast is particularly visible when one considers the claims made in *The Late Great Planet Earth* that the end will come "within forty years or so of 1948," the date of the reestablishment of Israel (p. 43). As Orson Welles intoned the message in the cinematic version of this book, "If the events in Revelation are truly prophetic, the remainder are to be fulfilled in our lifetime."

The issue to be dealt with here is not merely the stark contrast to the insistence of the historical Jesus, that "no one knows . . . but only the Father." The larger issue is how the Father himself is to be viewed. When the traditional message of doom is linked with the Father's will, God is thereby defined as the vindictive destroyer of the world. The Walvoords do not shrink from the awful implications of this view

in their book, *Armageddon: Oil and the Middle East Crisis.*
"In His first coming to earth, Jesus Christ was born in a
stable . . . in a time of comparative peace. . . . The second
coming of Jesus Christ to earth will be no quiet manger scene.
It will be the most dramatic and shattering event in the entire
history of the universe. . . . Cities will literally collapse,
islands sink, and mountains disappear. Huge hailstones, each
weighing a hundred pounds, will fall from heaven. . . . the
rulers and their armies who resist Christ's return will be
killed in a mass carnage." (Pp. 169–175.) Even Billy Graham
subscribes to this view of ultimate vindictiveness in *World
Aflame:* "God has offered his love and mercy and forgiveness
to men. . . . However, when that love is deliberately rejected,
the only alternative is judgment." (P. 218.)

The New Apocalypticism, committed to a schedule of
destruction that Jesus knew nothing about, derives its definition of God not from the authentic sayings and parables but
from the book of Revelation and other zealous strands of
Biblical thought. Thus our consideration of the end-time
prophecies must begin with the question of who the heavenly
Father really is. If the doctrine of God does not precede and
determine the shape of the end-time visions, it will be shaped
and determined by them. And although people may not be
conscious of it, this is precisely what happens in an era of
great apocalyptic tension. The father of all humankind comes
to be viewed in terms that were bluntly stated by the pub-
lisher of a "Christian Business Directory." As cited by William Simbro, he stated: "I believe God is a narrow-minded
God. Either you believe His way or you don't." And if you
don't, of course, the God of the New Apocalypticism will
shortly be aiming plagues and atomic conflagrations in your
direction. The question is whether such a God is the Father
of our Lord Jesus Christ.

I

In all the discussions of Mark 13:32–33 that I have examined, nowhere have I found a reference to what is surely a crucial point. The historical Jesus, since he spoke Aramaic and employed the term in a singular manner, would have used the word *abba* for "father." We have Joachim Jeremias to thank for raising our awareness of what this word implied. *Abba* was the term infants employed in addressing their male parent. Its more proper equivalent in current English would clearly be "Dad" or "Daddy." It was originally a babbling sound, far too immature, intimate, and childlike for use in prayer or theology. As Jeremias shows in *The Central Message of the New Testament,* "Jewish prayers . . . do not contain a single example of *abba* as an address for God; Jesus on the other hand always used it when he prayed (with the exception of the cry from the cross, Mark 15:34). . . . To a Jewish mind, it would have been irreverent and therefore unthinkable to call God by this familiar word. It was something new, something unique and unheard of, that Jesus dared to take this step and to speak with God as a child speaks with his father, simply, intimately, securely. There is no doubt then that the *Abba* which Jesus used to address God reveals the very basis of his communion with God." (Pp. 20f.)

To speak of God as Abba, therefore, conveys the sense that he is no longer stern and distant, but loving and close. Such speaking is possible only for those who feel unconditionally accepted by him and therefore dare to impose upon his lofty majesty with their childlike lisps. In fact, the saying "Unless you turn and become like children, you will never enter the kingdom of heaven" (Matt. 18:3) is clearly related to the Abba concept. As Jeremias writes in his *New Testament Theology,* " 'Become a child again' means: to learn to say *Abba* again" (p. 156). Only on the basis of grace is it possible to take this step. Early Christians who were far from the region where the word *abba* was used retained this sense of unconditional acceptance and connected it with the deepest level of religious experience. In Galatians and again in Romans, Paul explains the experience of the Spirit as a matter of God's evoking the cry of recognition of children to their Abba. "When we cry 'Abba! Father!' it is the Spirit himself bearing witness with our spirit that we are children of God." (Rom. 8:15–16.)

When Jesus insists that only the Abba knows the future, this sense of unconditional admission into the kingdom, of adoption as sons and daughters of God, is conveyed. Thus his use of the word *abba* reminds the disciples not only of the character of God but also of the nature of the future he intends to bring about. In view of the tradition of apocalyptic fury, vindictive judgment, and mean-spirited moralism of so large a part of the Judeo-Christian tradition, it is appropriate for us to review what Jesus himself said about the Abba. He is the one who acts mercifully, even to those who hate him (Luke 6:35–36). He listens to the prayers of his children, even when they lack eloquence or approved theology (Matt. 6: 6–8). He cares for all his creation, bedecking even the lilies of the pasture with beauty (Matt. 6:28–29) and noting even the sparrow's fall (Matt. 10:29). He far surpasses any earthly father in knowing the needs of his children and supplying them whether they deserve it or not (Luke 11:11–13). He is like the father who rejoices at the prodigal's return, not even requiring a proper act of repentance beforehand, who urges even the mean-spirited elder brother to join the festivities, lest any be excluded (Luke 15:11–32).

How does this powerful message about the Abba correspond with the vindictive threats of the New Apocalypticism? Are we to believe that the Abba's nature changes as the end of time draws near? That his mercy wears thin because the sins of moderns somehow exceed those of Sodom and Nineveh? That he who through patient aeons carved the depths of the Grand Canyon, and created the incredible bounty and beauty of this planet, would suddenly lose patience and destroy it all in an atomic conflagration? That humans are capable of such idiocy as this, I have no doubt.

But it is the farthest thing from the mind of the Abba who delights in crowning even the lowly grass with kingly blossoms. That is, if Jesus' message about the Abba is true.

The most eloquent depiction of an abba in recent American literature is found in Chaim Potok's *The Chosen.* It is the story of two sons growing to manhood in Brooklyn. They meet in a hard-fought and hateful baseball game in which Daniel Saunders, the brilliant son of the Hasidic master, Reb Saunders, literally tries to kill Reuven Malter by drilling a line drive straight over the pitcher's mound. It strikes Reuven in the face, driving a fragment of his shattered glasses into his eye. We are introduced to Reuven's father the day after the accident, when the narrator wakes up from the operation. Mr. Malter, of course, had spent a sleepless night by his unconscious son, who stands a good chance of losing his eyesight.

> I . . . saw a man hurrying up the aisle, and when he came into focus I saw it was my father. I almost cried out, but I held back and waited for him to come up to my bed. I saw he was carrying a package wrapped in newspapers. He had on his dark gray, striped, double-breasted suit and his gray hat. He looked thin and worn, and his face was pale. His eyes seemed red behind his steel-rimmed spectacles, as though he hadn't slept in a long time. He came quickly around to the left side of the bed and looked down at me and tried to smile. But the smile didn't come through at all.
>
> "The hospital telephoned me a little while ago," he said, sounding a little out of breath. "They told me you were awake."

Mr. Malter informs his son that the fragment of glass on the edge of the pupil has been removed, but the father looks worried.

> "Is the eye all right now?" I asked him.
> "Of course it is all right. Why should it not be all right?"
> "It's not all right," I said. "I want you to tell me."
> "There is nothing to tell you. They told me it was all right."
> "Abba, please tell me what's the matter."

He looked at me, and I heard him sigh. Then he began to
cough, a deep, rasping cough that shook his frail body terribly.
. . . I lay tense in the bed, watching him. The coughing stopped.
I heard him sigh again, and then he smiled at me. It was his old
smile, the warm smile that turned up the corners of his thin lips
and lighted his face.

"Reuven, Reuven," he said, smiling and shaking his head, "I
have never been good at hiding things from you, have I?" (Pp.
47–49)

Mr. Malter explained the uncertainty about whether the eye
would heal, and then unwrapped the package he had
brought. It was their only radio, to keep his son up on the
news about the war during the period when he would be
unable to read. " 'Very important things are happening,
Reuven,' he said, 'and a radio is a blessing.' He put the radio
on the night table. A radio brought the world together, he
said very often. Anything that brought the world together he
called a blessing." (P. 52.)

This tolerant trait of wanting to bring the world together
proves crucial for the story, because it turns out that Mr.
Malter had been the kindly, anonymous scholar in the stacks
of the public library who answered Danny Saunders' questions about what to read. He had been the one who discussed
the philosophical and psychological books the young genius
had devoured, forbidden readings from the perspective of the
Hasidim. His gentle advice and support proved to be crucial
in Danny's painful efforts to extricate himself from the domineering power of his father, the charismatic Reb Saunders.
But there are three occasions in the novel where patient,
long-suffering love gives way to anger at Reuven's tendency
to prejudge Danny Saunders and his difficult father. The first
of these occurred in the hospital room. Reuven states that
Danny had deliberately aimed the line drive at his head, that
he had made the game into a kind of holy war against heretics
like himself on the opposing team. He did not believe that
Reb Saunders had spoken truthfully on the phone to say his
son was sorry about the accident.

"Sorry! I'll bet he's sorry! He's sorry he didn't kill me altogether!"

My father gazed at me intently, his eyes narrowing. I saw the look of amazement slowly leave his face.

"I do not like you to talk that way," he said sternly.

"It's true, abba."

"Did you ask him if it was deliberate?"

"No."

"How can you say something like that if you are not sure? That is a terrible thing to say." He was controlling his anger with difficulty.

"It seemed to be deliberate."

"Things are always what they seem to be, Reuven? Since when?" I was silent.

"I do not want to hear you say that again about Reb Saunders' son."

"Yes, abba." (P. 51)

Urged by his father to give the relationship a chance, Reuven quickly becomes the best friend of his difficult antagonist, the tortured genius from a narrow-minded sect. Mr. Malter, who had kissed Reuven with red and misty eyes in the hospital while saying, "My baseball player," is able a few days later to say with his characteristic smile, "My two baseball players." (Pp. 53, 86.) Sustained by an abba's love, neither the heretic nor the heretic hater needs to be destroyed. Somehow they both belong to him.

II

Yet, if Jesus' unexpected saying is true, the heavenly Abba reserves the future for himself. He promises to fill all our legitimate needs—except the need to know. "No one knows," said Jesus with a finality that shocks the soothsayers of every generation. The force of this saying is diminished by its placement by Mark in a chapter full of traditional sayings about the end of the world, many of which lack the distinctive marks of original Jesus sayings. The scholarly consensus, as reported by Werner Kelber, is that Mark 13:5–31 contains material from a traditional Jewish-Christian apocalypse that flatly contradicts the authentic viewpoint of Jesus as articulated in vs. 32–37.

Even scholars who oppose this critical consensus are compelled by the evidence in our text to agree that it rejects any idea that the end can be calculated on the basis of apocalyptic signs. For example, speaking of Jesus' words in Mark 13:32 ("But of that day . . . no one knows"), C. E. B. Cranfield makes the following acknowledgment: "A clearer warning against all speculation about the *when* of the Parousia could hardly be imagined" (p. 411). The fact that this directly stated warning does not stand alone among the authentic Jesus sayings lends credence to its significance. For example, in Luke 17:20 Jesus replies to the request for an apocalyptic schedule: "The kingdom of God is not coming with signs to be observed." In Mark 8:12 he replied to the request for a sign from heaven with the flat answer: "No sign shall be given to this generation. . . ." We will subject this saying and its parallel in Matt. 16:1–4 to more detailed analysis in Chapter IV. These sayings denying knowledge of the end-time schedule are so dissimilar from the sayings of other apocalypticists in the ancient period that their authenticity is unquestionable. They are so scandalous an admission on the lips of Jesus that it is highly unlikely that the early church would have invented them.

The contrast with current statements of the New Apocalypticism could hardly be greater. Whereas Jesus insisted that "No one knows, not even the angels in heaven, nor the Son, but only the Father," Wilbur M. Smith wrote a book in 1971 entitled *You Can Know the Future.* There he states that, compared with the futile secular methods of forecasting the future, "there is only one divine book that contains a divine revelation, the Bible, . . . concerning the things that are to take place on this earth—your future, my future, the future of the nations of the earth, the future of Israel, the future of the world and the future of mankind." (P. 9.) By lumping Old and New Testament sayings together in an uncritical and unhistorical manner, Smith avoids the plain viewpoint of the historical Jesus. He moves through the customary scenes of the Antichrist, the Battle of Armageddon, and the Millennial kingdom without any hint of uncertainty. He writes as if he knew more than the angels and the Son combined.

In a similar vein, Ray C. Stedman's book, *What on Earth's Going to Happen?* opens with the appealing question, "How would you like to know the future?" He at least cites a version of the warning in Mark 13:33: "Watch, for you do not know when the time will come." But he places it on the same page with a statement that the "one unmistakable mark of the approaching end" is finally visible. Now that the gospel has been preached to all nations, the "near approach of the end" is visible. (P. 32.) Stedman is cagey enough to avoid setting a precise date as "some fanatics" have occasionally done. He states that "the day and the hour is clearly marked, 'Top Secret.' " Then he undercuts all this by stating on the same page: "We can know that the time is drawing near as we observe the predicted pattern taking place in the affairs of men" (p. 134).

There is a kind of apocalyptic inoculation at work among these writers, leading them to cite the authentic sayings of Jesus, but leaving them immune to their original meaning. One keeps on the safe side by acknowledging that the precise date of the end is unknown, while insisting on an apocalyptic program of annihilation utterly alien to the Abba whom Jesus proclaimed. David Wilkerson in *Racing Toward Judgment* denies that he is a "prophet" or a "Jeane Dixon" in the sense of making precise predictions about the future. But he opens his first chapter with the following lines adapted from Isaiah:

> Unbelievable disasters are roaring down upon us like a whirlwind from the outer limits of the universe. Awesome calamities will soon fall on this nation and mankind will be terrified. ... The upraised fist of God is poised, ready to destroy pride and to condemn the self-acclaimed greatness of our nation. (P. 9)

The power of inoculation is visible on a succeeding page when Wilkerson says: "[These] fearful judgments . . . will not all come immediately, but I believe they will all take place in our generation. We are on the brink of divine judgments so severe not one person will be left untouched." (P. 14.)

Perhaps the clearest example of this curious inoculation against the basic message of Jesus is found in a book entitled *God's Plan for the Future* by Lehman Strauss. "The exact time of the Rapture is not known. The setting of dates for this event has been one of the gross errors of which some teachers and writers have been guilty. However, though the exact time of Christ's coming for His Church is not known, we do not hesitate to state that we believe the Rapture is the next major event in God's prophetic program. The Translation of the Church to heaven is imminent." (P. 83.)

If citing Jesus' disclaimers seems to immunize current advocates of the New Apocalypticism against taking his message about the Abba seriously, one has to ask: Why is the state of apocalyptic certainty so appealing? When *Newsweek* reporter Kenneth Woodward and his colleagues investigated "The Boom in Doom," they found that "some expectant evangelicals appear positively cheerful in the face of Armageddon." They cite Pat Boone's comment: "My guess is that there isn't a thoughtful Christian alive who doesn't believe we are living at the end of history. . . . I don't know how that makes you feel, but it gets me pretty excited. Just think about actually seeing, as the apostle Paul wrote it, the Lord Himself descending from heaven with a shout! Wow! And the signs that it's about to happen are everywhere." (P. 51.) The appeal seems to be in knowing ahead of time what will happen, and anticipating that all one's expectations will soon be confirmed. It is as if one had seen a "sneak preview" of an important film, and now is in a position to be a step ahead of the miserable folks in the audience who are still worrying about whether the good guys will really win. Obviously there is not the slightest doubt in Boone's mind that he and his loved ones will be unscathed by the final conflagration. Nor, one must add with sadness, is there any sign of sympathy for the billions of men, women, and children whose lives will be snuffed out when the exciting nuclear battle begins.

The appeal of the New Apocalypticism is as old as mankind itself: to achieve mastery over a threatening future. It reaches back to the first reading of entrails or tea leaves, to the first gazing at the clouds and the position of the planets in an effort to grasp the future. Perhaps one should not be surprised by Pat Boone's obvious enthusiasm. But I have reflected for a number of years on the curious ordeal that Jesus underwent in the wilderness at the beginning of his ministry, and I had thought the implications were rather plain. He was taken in the temptation vision to the "pinnacle of the temple" and told: "If you are the Son of God, throw yourself down; for it is written, 'He will give his angels charge of you,' and 'On their hands they will bear you up, lest you strike your foot against a stone' " (Matt. 4:6). The action would have been parallel to his later career, for Jesus did throw down his life as a gauntlet in the cleansing of the Temple episode. The question was whether to seek the course of the future, to see ahead of time if a miracle of self-preservation would occur. The same kind of question obsessed the apocalyptic thinkers of Jesus' time: How to achieve certainty beforehand about the outcome of the struggle with the principalities and powers. The lure was to gain the sense of excitement every apocalypticist has in seeing his hopes confirmed in history. The odd thing was that Jesus perceived this central goal of the apocalyptics of his day as a demonic temptation. He replied, "You shall not put the Lord your God to the test," that is, you shall not demand sneak previews. You shall be content with the silence of the Abba about the course of the future. You shall "walk through the storm with your head up high, and not be afraid of the dark," to use the strangely appropriate lyrics from *Carousel.*

The theme of the Abba's silence is central to Potok's novel *The Chosen,* which casts a great deal of light on Jesus' perspective. Reb Saunders, the strange Hasidic master, used a method of silence in rearing his incredibly brilliant, and at times destructively headstrong, son. It was a medieval strata-

gem to teach future leaders of the sect to bear the pain of
loneliness, to look within themselves for strength, and to
trust in God rather than in human solace. The father would
discuss the Talmud with his son in ritualized sessions of
study and testing that would range over the vast memorized
terrain with ferocious mastery, probing for loopholes. But he
would not talk with him about the pains of growing to manhood. "We don't talk anymore," Danny Saunders confided
to his friend Reuven, "except when we study Talmud." (P.
160.) Reuven Malter reported this with indignation to his
father, who did not approve of this and many of the other
fanatical Hasidic traditions but would not bring himself to
condemn them. Reuven saw the terrible suffering his friend
was enduring, especially after Reb Saunders forbade the two
boys to associate because of Mr. Malter's Zionist activities.
Reuven found himself hating the bearded Rabbi and everything he stood for. "Silence was ugly, it was black, it leered,
it was cancerous, it was death. I hated it, and I hated Reb
Saunders for forcing it upon me and his son." (P. 221.)

In a climactic, revelatory scene, the great Talmudist explained why he had decided to use the silence in the rearing
of his beloved son. The conversation took place after Danny
had decided to break with the tradition of the Hasidic dy-
nasty, and to become a psychologist rather than the future
leader of the sect. Reb Saunders had aged terribly since
Reuven had last been allowed in his presence. He was
wracked by the agonies his people had undergone in the Nazi
death camps, and then by the news of battles and atrocities
connected with the establishment of the Zionist state, and
finally by illness in his family and the betrayal of his son. The
two boys sat by his desk in the book-lined study and the old
man sighed with "a deep, trembling sigh that filled the silence
of the room like a wind."

> "Nu, Reuven," he said quietly, "finally, finally you come to
> see me." He spoke in Yiddish, his voice quavering a little as the
> words came out.
> "I apologize," I said hesitantly, in English.

He nodded his head, and his right hand went up and stroked his gray beard. "You have become a man," he said quietly. "The first day you sat here, you were only a boy. Now you are a man."

It seemed that the rabbi could only speak to his son through his son's friend, so he continued.

"Reuven, the Master of the Universe blessed me with a brilliant son. And he cursed me with all the problems of raising him. . . . Ah, what a curse it is, what an anguish it is to have a Daniel, whose mind is like a pearl, like a sun. Reuven, when my Daniel was four years old, I saw him reading a story from a book. And I was frightened. He did not read the story, he swallowed it, as one swallows food or water. There was no soul in my four-year-old Daniel, there was only his mind. . . . It was a story in a Yiddish book about a poor Jew and his struggles to get to Eretz Yisroel before he died. Ah, how that man suffered! And my Daniel *enjoyed* the story, he *enjoyed* the last terrible page, because when he finished it he realized for the first time what a memory he had. He looked at me proudly and told me back the story from memory, and I cried inside my heart. I went away and cried to the Master of the Universe, 'What have you done to me? A mind like this I need for a son? A *heart* I need for a son, a *soul* I need for a son, *compassion* I want from my son, righteousness, mercy, strength to suffer and carry pain, *that* I want from my son, not a mind without a soul!' "

Reb Saunders paused and took a deep, trembling breath. I tried to swallow; my mouth was sand-dry. Danny sat with his right hand over his eyes, his glasses pushed up on his forehead. He was crying silently, his shoulders quivering. Reb Saunders did not look at him. (Pp. 262–264)

The old man went on to describe to Reuven how his own father had raised him in Poland, using the silence to teach him how to suffer and to find his own soul. "And it is important to know of pain," he would explain to those who inquired about the strange silence in the family. "It destroys our self-pride, our arrogance, our indifference toward others. It makes us aware of how frail and tiny we are and of how much we must depend upon the Master of the Universe."

Reb Saunders' mind flashed to scenes in which he had encountered the arrogance in his brilliant son. Danny, he recalled, "laughed once and said, 'That man is such an ignora-
mus, father!' I was angry. 'Look into his soul,' I said. 'Stand
inside his soul and see the world through his eyes. You will
know the pain he feels because of his ignorance, and you will
not laugh.' " Then Reb Saunders asked Reuven's forgiveness
for the period when he had been so outraged at his father's
Zionism. Finally he turned to his son:

> "Daniel," he said brokenly. "Forgive me . . . for everything
> . . . I have done. A—a wiser father . . . may have done differently.
> I am not . . . wise." (P. 268)

But the harsh silence has accomplished its deeper purpose,
for at the end of the novel, Danny Saunders is both free and
humane. His arrogance is gone, and he will use his mind in
the service of righteousness, fulfilling his father's hopes. For
he has learned to suffer, to share the uncertainty and the pain
that are the mark of our common humanity, no matter how
brilliant we are and regardless of the prophecies that have
been entrusted to our care.

And so it was with Jesus. Viewing God as the true Abba
who surpasses the wisdom and compassion of the most devoted human parents, he accepted and proclaimed the silence
about the most crucial question of all. "Though he was in the
form of God," sings the early Christian hymn, he "did not
count equality with God a thing to be grasped, but emptied
himself, taking the form of a servant, being born in the likeness of men" (Phil. 2:6f.). He submitted to the silence until,
in the cry of forsakenness on the cross, he tasted the plight
of all humankind. As the Epistle to the Hebrews confesses,
Jesus died that he might "taste death for every one," sharing
our limitations "in every respect" (Heb. 2:9, 17).

Shall we do less for each other? Is it right that we, the
children of the heavenly Abba, should pretend that we know
the future, that we can penetrate the divine silence, and thus
that we are superior to others? Are we now to fall prey to the

arrogant exultation of those who presume that the future is
somehow working out according to our formulas, and that
the tribulations of our day follow a design to prove our
superior knowledge? No. The Abba's love is enough for us
even in the thick of silence. It sustains us through all uncer-
tainties, even through death itself. The silence has a purpose
deeper than we can know, to protect our humanity. We do
not know the day or the hour; we cannot know the year or
even the century; but we are not condemned to despair.
While he holds us in communion, the Abba's silence guards
us from the future, that we might truly be his children who
can bear one another's burdens.

III

The unexpected prophecy is therefore a call to "watch" in
the silence. "Take heed, watch; for you do not know when
the time will come. . . . Watch therefore—for you do not
know when the master of the house will come. . . . And what
I say to you I say to all: Watch!" (Mark 13:33–37.) To watch
is to be prepared for the unexpected. It is to give up the
illusions of straight-line extrapolations, the silly assumption
that current trends will continue. It is to abandon the calculations of the pundits about the swinging of some invisible
pendulum. In this time, particularly, it is to accept the fact
that life will not go on as it has. A change is in the offing, but
no one knows what direction it will take. History is the realm
of contingency, the unexpected. The proper eschatology is
watchful expectancy for the Abba's work and will, and a
wary guardedness about the rebounding perversity of
humankind. The danger is to preempt the future with our
own agenda and our own eagerness to be proven right by
history.

At this point the strange inoculation of the New Apocalypticism causes an outrageous turn. Whereas Jesus taught
watchfulness because "you do *not* know when the time will
come," *The Late Great Planet Earth* teaches us to scout for

every indication that we *do* possess the secret formula. It leads us to welcome every atrocity, to delight in every evidence of ecological decline, to exult at every sign of earthquake and hail, and to rejoice as our brothers in Africa and the Middle East move ever closer to the brink of World War III. The most horrible events are welcomed as signs that the end is in sight, that we shall shortly be raptured from this vale of tearful uncertainty, and that the willfully unenlightened will soon receive their just deserts. For the devotees of the New Apocalypticism, the most appalling news simply proves that they are right. As David Wilkerson insists in *Racing Toward Judgment,* Christians should thank God for the "Bad News That Is Really Good News." "Those who believe the Bible understood that all these things must come to pass before the end comes. Christians rejoice because all the bad news is a series of signposts clearly marked out on their roadmap to eternity. Each terrifying event more clearly pinpoints our position down the homestretch." (P. 138.)

Such sentiments are a continent removed from the attitude of children waiting expectantly for the Abba's surprising future. One reason God reserves it in silence is that we are thereby enabled to greet it freshly, to taste his grace in the new dawn of every day, to experience his love anew with each breath of air. Genuine living is response to the unexpected. The parables of Jesus teach an expectant aliveness, a readiness to live intensely in the now, while giving up all our efforts to control tomorrow. When the "pearl of great price" is offered, it must be purchased "at once"; when the invitation to the banquet arrives, it must be accepted no matter how disreputable one's dinner partners turn out to be. The Abba always surprises us, and to live as his children means sitting expectantly on the edge of our seats, waiting to see what happens next. It means giving full attention to today's task, heed to our present conversation partners, responsiveness to the genuine "news," whatever it happens to be.

Especially on this final point, the Judaic material in Chaim Potok's novel can serve to sharpen and deepen our grasp of the unexpected message of Jesus. I mentioned earlier that

Reuven's father became angry on several occasions in the story; two of these related to not "listening" or "watching" in response to human need. After the injured boy had spurned the apology of Danny Saunders, who paid him a visit in the hospital to see how the eye was healing, he described the encounter to his father. He had told Danny to go "to hell, and take your whole snooty bunch of Hasidim along with you"; that he didn't want to "listen" to anything he had to say. The eyes of Reuven's kindly father "became angry behind the glasses" at this report.

> "You did a foolish thing, Reuven," he told me sternly. "You remember what the Talmud says. If a person comes to apologize for having hurt you, you must listen and forgive him."
>
> "I couldn't help it, abba."
>
> "You hate him so much you could say those things to him?"
>
> "I'm sorry," I said, feeling miserable.
>
> He looked at me and I saw his eyes were suddenly sad. "I did not intend to scold you," he said.
>
> "You weren't scolding," I defended him.
>
> "What I tried to tell you, Reuven, is that when a person comes to talk to you, you should be patient and listen. Especially if he has hurt you in any way." (Pp. 63f.)

On the final occasion in the novel, Reuven's hatred for the domineering Reb Saunders, and his supposition about what the old man would do, kept him from listening again. In the months before the climactic conversation in Reb's study, the request came repeatedly for Reuven to pay him a visit. The young man was deeply immersed in his college studies, and was certain from his bitter stereotype of the Hasidic master that he only wanted him to come so that they could "study Talmud" again together. Then Reuven told his father about the invitation to come to the Saunders house on the first or second day of Passover. There was a "strange sharpness" in his father's reply.

> "You did not tell me Reb Saunders has been asking to see you."

"He's been asking all along."

"Reuven, when someone asks to speak to you, you must let him speak to you. . . . You have not been listening."

When the young man attempts to place the visit on his own time schedule, his father insists he submit to the terms of the invitation.

"You will go on Passover. He has a reason if he asked you to come especially on Passover. And listen next time when someone speaks to you, Reuven."

He was angry, as angry as he had been in the hospital years ago when I had refused to talk to Danny. (P. 258)

To take heed and watch is to listen as well. It is to attend to the demands of the present moment as if they were the Abba's urging, and to respond with equal intensity when we are confronted with an entirely new situation on the morrow. It is *his* future we are to expect, not one that matches our narrow hopes and stifled stereotypes, for the ultimate purpose of the Abba's silence is to set us free—free from the burden of the past and from ourselves. As the aging Reb Saunders said to the two stunned young men at the conclusion of the Passover interview: "Today is the—the Festival of Freedom. . . . Today my Daniel is free. . . ." It was said with "a soft hint of bitterness" by a disappointed, yet profoundly wise father. (P. 268.) But in the larger world—where, only the Abba knows—such liberation is basic. The final lines of Potok's novel convey something of this freedom in the Abba's open future, as Daniel Saunders, now committed to a mature faith, capable of compassion, and eager for his new profession, disappears around the corner onto Lee Avenue.

"I watched him walk quickly away, tall, lean, bent forward with eagerness and hungry for the future." (P. 271)

For us as Christians, it is a future that only the Abba knows. Let us watch, therefore, for every occasion of his coming, holding ourselves ready for his word, and for every urging of his spirit. "Watch, therefore," for the future that "only the Abba knows."

Chapter II

Falling like Lightning from Heaven

Luke 10:17–20

The element of the unexpected is basic to Jesus' prophecies. Jesus used the metaphor of an unpredictable lightning flash in response to the amazing report of the disciples about their success in proclaiming the kingdom of God. "Lord, even the demons are subject to us in your name!" (Luke 10:17.) Jesus' reply about the lightning bolt was couched in a past tense that has always seemed curiously out of place: "I saw Satan fall like lightning from heaven," Jesus said (Luke 10:18). The unexpected quality of the flashing image is clear, especially in an environment like Palestine, where electrical storms are comparatively rare. While thunder follows lightning with predictable regularity, there was no way for ancients to forecast when lightning would strike. But why did Jesus say he "saw" the fall of Satan, as if it were an event of the past? What connection did this have with the exorcisms performed by his disciples and with the triumph of the good news? And given the centrality of this theme in current end-of-time predictions, all of which place the demise of Satan in the future as a result of a final battle, what is the significance of Jesus' vision for our time?

I

Not long after I received the invitation to the Jerusalem conference, an article arrived that cleared up the mystery of the saying about Satan falling like lightning. Ulrich B. Müller, a professor of New Testament in a West German university, showed that Jesus' saying was similar to the prophetic visions of Amos, Jeremiah, Isaiah, and Ezekiel. Apparently an actual vision occurred early in his ministry in which Satan was seen to be cast down from heaven without any human assistance. "The fall of Satan thereby derives from God's action. . . . An action of Jesus or his disciples is not in view." (P. 418.) The authenticity of this saying is enhanced by the fact that none of the apocalyptic writings in Jesus' time or before had depicted such an occurrence as already accomplished. Müller cites a number of statements in the Dead Sea Scrolls and elsewhere that predict a future defeat of Satan and his forces, usually as a result of an apocalyptic battle. Even the book of Revelation departs from Jesus at this point. It pictures the casting down of Satan and his angels as a future event rather than one already accomplished (Rev. 12:7–9). So unique and incredible was Jesus' vision that even a Christian writer like John found it preferable to revert to the traditional apocalypticism. This reversion in the book of Revelation is followed by end-of-time visionaries down to our present day.

The vision of Satan's fall, according to Müller, was directly related to Jesus' proclamation of the presence of the kingdom of God. Scholars have long observed that Jesus had a peculiar combination of the present and the future in his kingdom sayings. Now was the time for celebration instead of fasting, Jesus taught, because the messianic bridegroom is present (Mark 2:19). Yet the disciples are to pray for the coming of the kingdom (Matt. 6:10). The key to understanding this is the premise of Satan's fall. What others had expected as a result of a future Battle of Armageddon, Jesus saw as already having occurred. Since Satan's power has already been broken, the kingdom is available here and now. When this message was accepted by those who formerly assumed that Satan was in control of the world, the kingdom's triumph would be complete.

Jesus' belief in the presence of the kingdom of God distinguished his message from that of John the Baptist. Müller draws some wide-ranging conclusions about this. "What separated Jesus from the Baptist is his faith that the end must not only be expected soon . . . but that in the fall of Satan a final event had already occurred. Thereafter the power of God's rule can be experienced as present in the action of Jesus." (P. 426.) While John's baptism offered safety from the wrath to come, Jesus' vision was that the wrath was already over: the fearsome battle against Satan had already been won, and hence the earth was the Lord's. Müller connects this with Jesus' break with the Mosaic law in the "But I say unto you" passages. The fall of Satan ushered in a new period in which a new ethic was appropriate. Finally, Müller links the vision with Jesus' unusual attitude toward nature. He alone among the thinkers of his time drew radical ethical consequences from natural phenomena like rain and sunshine falling equally on the evil and the good. Since Satan has been dethroned, the natural world no longer needs to be viewed as corrupt and embodying principles of retribution. As Müller puts it, "The creation moves toward its de-demonization since Satan's power is challenged" (p. 441). Therefore one can begin to dare to love one's enemies (Matt. 5:44–48), since they are children of the same heavenly Father rather than agents of some demonic campaign. One can confidently accept and live with sinners, since they lack the demonic power to corrupt and lead astray. Hence one can also cease worrying about being corrupted by nonkosher foods, since the demonic cannot enter from without (Mark 9:15).

None of these radical ideas was conceivable for other teachers of Jesus' time—even though the idea of the divine creation of the world was generally assumed—because the notion of Satan's dominance over the present produced a kind of practical dualism. The vision of Satan's fall made all the difference, allowing Jesus to reclaim nature and history as free from demonic compulsion and hence as arenas for human responsibility.

II

Once we have understood the revolutionary significance of Jesus' vision of Satan falling like lightning, its relations to the report of successful exorcisms and to our present moment become clear. The disciples had returned from their mission to spread the good news to "the lost sheep of the house of Israel" (Matt. 10:6) with a report of marvelous success. As Luke 10:17 describes it, they had returned to their Master "with joy" because the harvest he had promised was so plentiful. The revival was on, just as it is in our time. The impact of the gospel surpassed their highest hopes. Even in cases where demonic compulsion threatened to keep people from responding with a balanced mind, the disciples had amazing successes to report: "Lord, even the demons are subject to us in your name!" When Jesus replied that he had seen Satan "fall like lightning from heaven," the effect was explanatory. As J. M. Creed writes, "The defeat of Satan explains the success of the disciples" (p. 147). The past tense of the verb makes it clear that Jesus did not view the exorcisms themselves as constituting the fall of Satan. Since the fall had already occurred, the exorcisms were to be viewed as the joyous freeing of prisoners after an evil adversary had collapsed.

The connection between these verses throws a completely new light on the healings that Jesus and his disciples are known to have performed. The theme of violent combat between Jesus and the demonic realm is a prominent feature of Mark's Gospel, as James M. Robinson and other analysts of the Gospel viewpoints have shown. Recent novels and films like *The Exorcist* and *The Omen* enhance this popular vision of fierce struggle against an immensely powerful demonic realm. But if Jesus' vision is as crucial as it appears to be, his exorcisms had much more nearly the character of demolishing a house of cards. Since Satan had already fallen, his uncanny power was already broken. He was now a crippled adversary, evoking fear and despair because people continued to believe what was no longer true. Despite the vivid imagination of men, even of Gospel writers like Mark, Satan no longer had the world under his control. This correlates well with the calm and businesslike manner in which Jesus conducted exorcisms, even in Mark's most dramatic accounts. There is none of the blood, sweat, and agony of *The Exorcist* in any of the Gospel accounts.

This explains also why Jesus constantly stressed faith as the key to successful exorcisms. It was not a matter of magical belief or superstitious power. To have faith in Jesus' sense was to believe in the power of God as manifest in his kingdom, and to know that a fallen Satan could no longer prevail in the lives of God's children. That is why Jesus insisted that the amount of human faith was irrelevant for exorcisms: faith the size of a mustard seed would suffice if Satan had already fallen. This is not to say that human resistance and the peculiarities of specific maladies could be disregarded. As Jesus explained when his disciples were unable to heal the convulsive child, "This kind cannot be driven out by anything but prayer" (Mark 9:29). A specific kind of mental energy was required in the face of that particular disease, but Jesus does not even hint that Satan had somehow returned to his position of power. The statement about faith addressed to the child's father is the same here as everywhere, "All things are possible to him who believes" (Mark 9:23). The sweeping quality of this claim has its basis in the vision of Satan's demise.

An unfortunate feature of the current religious revival is that many of those most committed to Jesus' kind of exorcisms turn his viewpoint upside down. Whereas Jesus perceived the fall of Satan as the premise of human redemption, they proclaim belief in Satan's continued power as the essential first step in becoming a disciple. In A.D. 30 or so, Jesus declared that Satan had fallen from his powerful throne, but in A.D. 1972 Hal Lindsey wrote a book entitled *Satan Is Alive and Well on Planet Earth.* He has since reiterated the claim in *The Liberation of Planet Earth* that "Satan calls the shots over this present world system" (p. 58). Without taking into account Jesus' authentic saying in Luke 10:18, Lindsey makes as sweeping a case for faith in Satan as any of the apocalyptic writers in the ancient period. Since Adam and Eve succumbed to Satan's wiles, he writes, "they unwittingly turned over their God-given power and authority to Satan's control. He became the legal controller of all men who would ever be born from Adam's seed. He also took control of the planet itself and all creation on it, animal and vegetable. . . . This sellout of Adam to Satan is how the world got into the mess it's in today. With Satan as the legal ruler of this planet, it became one great big slave market and everyone born into it of Adam's seed is born a slave of Satan. This was clearly taught by Jesus and His disciples." (P. 57.)

Taught by some of his disciples, to be sure, but not by Jesus himself. Perhaps the most contradictory aspect of such statements is that they come from latter-day disciples who claim to follow literally every single word Jesus taught. If Lindsey were to catch his Master's vision of that flashing and disappearing streak of electricity, he would have to revise his entire outlook. It is not Satan, but God who is alive and well on planet Earth.

III

Increasing numbers of Americans are coming to the conclusion that Jesus in effect was wrong about the demise of Satan. In the years since 1964 the percentage of Americans who believe that Satan is alive and well has dramatically increased. In a recent article Clyde Z. Nunn describes the "Rising Credibility of the Devil in America." His study shows that when compared with 1964, the percentage of Americans in 1973 who were "absolutely certain that the

Devil exists increased from 37 percent to 50 percent. Another
21 percent in 1973 thought that it was probably true that the
Devil exists." (P. 84.) According to this study, 71 percent of
Americans are convinced—or at least fairly sure—that the
devil is alive and well. One of the remarkable features of this
statistic is that it occurs at a time when belief in God is
gradually declining within the culture as a whole.

The studies of the Center for Policy Research, which
Nunn reports, do not indicate that belief in Satan is rising
because of adherence to Satanistic cults. The belief in the
devil is not concentrated in the tiny circles of Satan worshipers but overwhelmingly in church people. In fact, the survey
showed that "among the most active religious attenders,
. . . 83 percent believed it was completely true that the Devil
exists. As frequency of attendance declined, certainty of the
Devil's existence declined." (P. 87.) The organized church,
therefore, must be given primary responsibility for having
popularized a belief diametrically opposed to that advocated
by its Master. The mood of our era also contributes to belief
in Satan, according to Nunn and his associates. The study
explains the rise in the credibility of the devil on the basis of
the increasing sense of the failure and breakdown of society
in the last decade. "The Devil is seen as the source of failure
and imperfections (evils) in the society" (p. 91). This is sustained by the fact that there is a high correlation between
belief in God and belief in the devil; those who believe in God
also were seen by the poll to be strongly committed to social
order and worried about threats to it. "When life is believed
to be falling apart, the Devil is given equal or greater credibility than God" (p. 94).

With the widespread sense that the forces of chaos, crime,
and exploitation are gaining ascendancy, our era assumes a
striking similarity to the first century. As now, it seemed very
natural to perceive Satan's hand in daily frustrations, to sense
his spirit animating one's enemies. This helped to justify
violence against adversaries, because if Satan were in control,
any means to counter his realm would be justified. Since
demonic enemies could not be converted, they would have to

be destroyed. The vicious intolerance of Jesus' day was fueled by the conviction that Satan was alive and well on planet earth.

Consistent with his vision of the demise of Satan, Jesus sought to counter the trends toward intolerance, hatred, and violent crusading. The parable of the tares, for instance, urged the forsaking of human crusades against weeds that some demonic "enemy" had presumably planted. The good wheat would inevitably be rooted up in the process (Matt. 13:24–30). Jesus advocated an approach to kingdom membership that tolerantly goes beyond the question of eliminating Satanic neighbors: the fishnet of the kingdom swept in both the good and the bad, while leaving to the angels at the end of time the superhuman task of discrimination (Matt. 13:47–50). Jesus understood that tolerance, mutual respect, and love were impossible as long as one saw Satan occupying the neighbor's house.

The rising credibility of the devil in America today is cause for alarm because it undercuts the entire ethic of tolerant love that Jesus brought to the world. The Nunn study shows a striking correlation between intolerance and belief in the devil. It found that "those lowest in tolerance of nonconformists are the most certain about the Devil (73 percent). Those most tolerant are least likely to be certain the Devil exists (35 percent)." Nunn's book, *Tolerance for Nonconformity,* develops this point in more extensive detail. The entire democratic heritage of equality before the law, the presumption of innocence before being proven guilty, due process of law, and fair trial in the courts is jeopardized by militant belief in Satan's power over human behavior. The route leading from a declaration that Satan is alive and well on planet earth to burning his presumed witches as agents of demonic power is straight and logical.

Paul Johnson's eloquent *History of Christianity* provides a reminder of where belief in Satan leads. During the bitter struggles between Catholics and Protestants, witchcraft terror reached its peak in Western civilization. "Luther thought that witches should be burnt for making a pact with the Devil even if they harmed no one, and he had four of them roasted at Wittenberg. . . . The Calvinists, in fact, were much fiercer against witches than the Lutherans. . . . Then, with the Catholic reconquest of Bohemia and parts of Germany, the witch-trials multiplied. This last great phase of witch-hunting was the product of Catholic-Protestant rivalry, since hunters on both sides often identified witchcraft with opposing beliefs. . . . Philip Adolf von Ehrenberg, Bishop of Wurtzburg, burned over 900 during his reign 1623–31, including his own nephew, nineteen priests and a child of seven. In the Bavarian prince-bishopric of Eichstatt, 274 were burned in the year 1629 alone. . . . The worst hunt of all was at Bamberg, where the 'witch-bishop,' Johann Georg II Fuchs von Dornheim burned 600 witches, 1623–33. His chancellor, accused of leniency, implicated under torture five burgomasters; one of them, arrested and tortured in turn, accused twenty-seven colleagues, but later managed to smuggle out a letter to his daughter: 'It is all falsehood and invention, so help me God. . . . They never cease to torture until one says something. . . . If God sends no means of bringing the truth to light, our whole kindred will be burned.' " (Pp. 309–311.) The tragedy of Christian history is that the truth in a larger sense was brought to light at the very beginning, in the indelible memory of a lightning flash across the Galilean sky. But the significance of this vision has repeatedly been obscured in troubled times by the resurgence of popular superstition.

It is important to understand that what has been observed thus far does not deny the reality of the demonic. How can the immense evil of the twentieth century, with its death camps, torture cells, and atomic rubble, be comprehended without some idea of the demonic? How can the broad strand of Biblical witness be comprehended when it affirms the reality of Satanic possession? As a matter of fact, Jesus' vision does not lead to the denial of the existence of the demonic. It leads instead to a revision of prevailing views of its location, and a restraint of any idea of its continuing supernatural sway. When Jesus' position as a whole is pieced together, it comes remarkably close to Ernest Becker's perspective in

Angel in Armor. "The Demonic is real," this psychoanalytic theorist insists, but it does not consist of some superhuman force. "It comes into being when men fail to act *individually* and *willfully,* on the basis of their own *personal, responsible* powers. The Demonic refers specifically to the creation of power by groups of men who blindly follow authority and convention, power which then engulfs them and defeats them. Let us also note that The Demonic has a naturalistic basis. It comes into being on the basis of a real evolutionary development: man is the animal in nature who, par excellence, can create vast structures of power by means of his symbolic manipulation of the world of energy . . . [which] become enslaving over the very individuals who contribute to their creation: the group dominates the individual, and the leaders manipulate the groups." (P. 111.)

Whenever we give in to the temptation to say, "They forced me into this situation," or "The System gave me no choice," or "The Devil made me do it," the demonic springs to life out of our denial of responsibility. It is humans who create and even at times embody the demonic, as the remarkable exchange between Peter and Jesus at Caesarea Philippi reveals. The disciple had upbraided his Master for planning to return to Jerusalem in the face of certain death. He did not want to share the risks of facing down the power structures, preferring no doubt that angelic forces should come first to smash some demonic strongholds. But Jesus "turned and said to Peter, 'Get behind me, Satan! You are a stumbling block to me, for you are not on the side of God, but of men' " (Matt. 16:23). This statement cannot be comprehended on the basis of the traditional concept of demonic possession. Rather than being controlled by Satan, Peter *becomes* Satan in the act of evading responsibility to cope with evil directly and personally. It was a cop-out similar to that encouraged by the New Apocalypticism, which assumes that we are powerless to avert the drift to catastrophe. Since Satan is alive and well, we can do nothing but wait for the Rapture to release us from his wiles.

If the unexpected prophecy of Jesus is correct, Satan

becomes alive and well only when humans evade the exercise of their powers and cower before institutions, public opinion, and seemingly uncanny destiny. But since the mythological Satan made his final flash downward against the sky, God's will is for humans to come of age, to shoulder their responsibilities, and to prevail.

IV

The verse that follows the report of Satan's fall emphasizes the power of Jesus' disciples over formerly enchanted realms: "Behold, I have given you authority to tread upon serpents and scorpions, and over all the power of the enemy; and nothing shall hurt you" (Luke 10:19). The context should be carefully noted, lest the bold promise be taken to imply a new realm of magical immunity. It is defined by Satan's fall, not by some concern about venomous reptiles. Jesus' stress on the demystification of the demonic is picked up by the expression "over all the power of the enemy." Jesus did not have in mind immunity to snakebite, but rather boldness in the face of the Satanic power, which had been thought to animate "serpents and scorpions." The wording is influenced by the apocalyptic expectation that when the messianic age arrived, even a child could play over the adder's den (cf. Isa. 11:8). Jesus is suggesting that this was fulfilled by the collapse of Satan's realm.

The secondary ending to Mark's Gospel reveals that Jesus' saying was badly misinterpreted by at least one branch of the early church. The idea of power over serpents is taken in the superstitious direction favored by the Appalachian snake-handling churches of more recent times: "And these signs will accompany those who believe: in my name they will cast out demons; they will speak in new tongues; they will pick up serpents, and if they drink any deadly thing, it will not hurt them; they will lay their hands on the sick, and they will recover" (Mark 16:17–18). When promises like this are interpreted without reference to the fall-of-Satan vision, they lead to conclusions that are the exact opposite of those taught by Jesus. The snake-handling cults, through a similar misunderstanding, assume that the demonic realm of serpenthood is still intact, but that they have been given a magical immunity through faith. The founder of a snake-handling cult in Tennessee, George Went Hensley, began by seeking a demonstration of his faith and salvation. Carl Glassman reports that the members of the cult "believe that they alone are entitled to salvation" (p. 23). The movement has declined since Hensley was bitten at a Florida prayer meeting in 1955, but the misunderstanding is basic. Jesus had no need for this kind of shallow and risky superstition. If Satan had really fallen, humankind was free to approach snakes as snakes without assuming they are connected with some realm of supernatural power. There is nothing demonic about venom.

Rather than encouraging superstitions about snake-handling, Jesus' intent in Mark 16:15 was to encourage a fearless responsibility for the world. The emphasis is on the "authority" of disciples "over all the power of the enemy" (Luke 10:19), which the superstitious first century had thought was concentrated in reptiles. Since Satan had now been deposed, it followed that his "power" was eliminated. The whole realm of nature was thereby disenchanted, and Jesus' followers are to approach it without fear. We have in this verse an essential component of the scientific world view that was later to arise on Christian soil. So long as nature remained enchanted with malevolent and unpredictable powers, scientific investigation could not develop. And when in the twentieth century more and more people are becoming convinced of uncanny forces, whether satanic or ecological, acting with vast powers to frustrate any human effort, this entire legacy is undermined. Fear of the supernatural begins to creep in to erode human responsibility. Who will dare to contend with problems that are caused by supernatural powers? In Luke 10:19 Jesus set forth the basis for overcoming the superstitious world view that has afflicted humankind repeatedly since the dawn of civilization. Its relevance for us is obvious: we are to go about coping with the complex dilemmas of nature and history in the confidence that nothing uncanny "shall hurt" us. The mistakes we make will be our own; the forces we unleash will have their own comprehensible laws; and the ends to which our science is directed are of our own choosing. They are in our "authority."

This verse counters a decisive motivation in the perennial credibility of the devil—the feeling of powerlessness. Clyde Nunn's studies indicate a correlation between belief in the devil and disbelief in human powers. The highest levels of belief in the devil are found in those portions of our population that feel least able to contend with the complexities of modern life. The feeling that someone else is in control and that there is nothing one can do about it is surfacing more and more in the popular culture of the last several decades. The catastrophe films portray superhuman forces at work that are far beyond the capacities of average citizens or normal governmental agencies to control. Films like *Taxi Driver* depict urban corruption on a scale that finally defeats life, lending plausibility to the final paroxysm of violence against those who appear responsible. The widely read novels of Joseph Heller and Kurt Vonnegut, Jr., depict senseless organizations drifting so far out of human control that laughter at such absurdity seems to be the only suitable response.

For many Christians, the attributing of vast supernatural powers to Satan is a reaction to a pervasive sense of powerlessness. After discussing this passage and its implications with an audience recently, I was approached by a minister who reported that the concept of a personal devil had once been crucial to his faith. It seemed to provide a kind of solace for the deep sense of personal inadequacy he felt in his ministry and in his personal life. As he matured, however, and discovered in the grace of God the power to accept himself despite feelings of inferiority, his interest in the concept of Satan gradually diminished. Particularly as he developed more competent counseling techniques, he found he was able to minister to people without resorting to the idea of the devil. He observed that as the members of his congregation gained a fuller sense of the acceptance and authority in Christ, they also found themselves setting aside the credibility of Satan. Thus the logic of Jesus' unexpected prophecy is borne out in the life of faith.

V

The final verse in our passage, Luke 10:20, announces a theme that is central for this entire investigation of Jesus' end-time sayings. It establishes a proper relation between prophecy, exorcism, and the kingdom of God. Jesus warned his disciples not to rejoice "that the spirits are subject to you," but rather "that your names are written in heaven." He was pointing to the centrality of the kingdom relationship. To have your name in the heavenly book is to be a fully accepted member of the kingdom of God. The "rejoicing" he had in view in Luke 10:20 was the same as that occasioned by the return of the prodigal son, the recovery of the lost coin, the finding of the pearl of great price. The key to "rejoicing" is the new relationship with God. It is not a reward for obedience, as much Christian preaching and writing maintains. To speak of rejoicing about one's heavenly reward for good behavior is a serious distortion of Jesus' distinctive message about the kingdom of heaven. Unearned grace is the only basis of admission into the kingdom. It precedes repentance, and it evokes the kind of joy that is the sign of a new life.

Still, it may seem puzzling that Jesus found it necessary to conclude his explanation about the success of the disciples' exorcisms with this warning, beginning with "Nevertheless." Does it not seem strange that he would dampen their enthusiasm about the tremendous success of their mission? What sales executive would say such a thing after his representatives return with stunning accounts of success? I think the answer lies in Jesus' perception that rejoicing at the wrong things can hinder the growth of disciples toward genuine maturity. To rejoice that the spirits are subject to your control is to rejoice in your own power, in your charisma, while

serving as a channel for the triumph of God. It is to take
primary delight in the possession of power. The trouble is
that power always corrupts. To adapt the rule of experience
in politics to the area of ministry: absolute charismatic power
corrupts absolutely. It develops the sense of superiority over
others; it encourages the narcissistic tendencies latent in everyone; and it hinders the growth of realistic self-knowledge
that is indispensable to continued maturation.

Temptations in the exercise of superhuman powers are
constantly set forth in the popular entertainments of our
time. Since the 1930's, the patterns of American heroism
have changed in the direction of superheroism. Figures like
Superman, Wonder Woman, Captain Marvel, or Captain
America, whose distinguishing mark is the possession of
superhuman strength or invulnerability, have been followed
in recent years by the Bionic Man and the Bionic Woman.
The incredible powers of these fantasy figures to help others
and to overcome uncanny enemies are deeply appealing to
the immature. To possess such powers is to rise above human
limitations; it is to earn the accolades of rescued maidens and
cheering crowds. But the fantasy world of such stories always
obscures the basic realities of power. The fiction of pure
innocence is maintained so that power never corrupts the
Lone Ranger or Steve Austin. They are portrayed as never
taking pleasure in the gratitude of those they redeem; they
never change as the years and the episodes go by. In real life,
however, power corrupts, and the cheers of crowds go to the
head and heart of heroes. Still, millions of Americans yearn
for the fantasy of superhuman powers to become reality.
They sit glued to the television set while the dramas roll by,
and they collect the comic books or fan magazines about the
stars with a kind of fanatical devotion. In the era of punk
rock music, adolescents sit in their rooms, strumming clum-
sily on guitars and dreaming of becoming superstars. They
yearn for the time when they will be applauded by the world
and have their anonymity and poverty overcome.

A more realistic picture of the impact of superhuman
powers on humans would prevail if current Americans took

more seriously the tragic lives of their entertainment heroes. Perhaps movies like *A Star Is Born* have some sobering effect. They relate the story of the disintegration of character, the lapse into drugs and alcohol, the disruption of marriage and other basic human relationships, and the often successful flirtation with death. The mortality rate of the superstars of rock, film, and television appears to match the opportunity to abuse their human powers, stretching them beyond human limits and resulting in despair over the meaning of life. To rejoice in the exercise of one's powers is a sure route to egocentric emptiness. It is to place one's feet on the slippery path toward oblivion.

The realm of entertainment fantasies is simply the most visible embodiment of a perennial law of human nature that is reflected in Luke 10:20. To rejoice in mastery of any type is not conducive to human growth and balance. Hence Jesus suggests that the appropriate center for the rejoicing of his disciples should be the new relationship in the kingdom of God. Whereas the exercise of power elevates and isolates the self from others, the kingdom relationship is one of equality. If we are accepted into the kingdom regardless of our accomplishments, we remain equal in God's sight and, as we continue internalizing the gospel, equal in our own sight as well. In place of the mastery and manipulation of others, a greater delight develops in participation with others. Cooperation and mutual support begin to emerge as the more mature grounds for rejoicing. The kingdom community is marked neither by domination nor adulation of the powerful, but rather by the free development of the unique talents of each individual. The name of each is known and cherished in the kingdom's book. To be thus known and accepted is the solid basis for each to give up pretenses and accomplishments for the sake of a common cause.

The final verse of this unexpected prophecy thus places the spiritual revival reported by the disciples in perspective, and carries out in a logical manner the thrust of the fall-of-Satan vision. It now becomes apparent that the reason Jesus reported his remarkable vision at this point was to clarify the basis of the disciples' amazing success in such a way that the aftermath would not be destructive. Were the disciples to conclude that their own charisma was the decisive channel for the defeat of Satan, they would not only gain a false sense of their position as humans beings but would fall into the power trap that universally afflicts the successful. The triumph, as Luke 10:18 explains, was due, not to their charisma at all, but rather to the fall of Satan from his position of power. To adhere to this line is not only to find a center in the relationship with a gracious Abba but to move out into mature responsibility for his world.

Chapter III

The Inverted Kingdom

Luke 4:16–30

Throughout the world today a mighty upsurge of the Spirit is being felt. New groups are being formed inside and outside the churches of North America. New vitality is visible in the churches of Africa and South America. New signs of life are reported in South Korea, India, and the Philippines. Miracles of healing and transformation are being reported on every side. In the summer of 1977, the largest ecumenical gathering of charismatics in American history took place in Kansas City. Fifty thousand Christians from dozens of denominations crowded into Arrowhead Stadium to sing hymns like "Come, Holy Ghost." Kenneth A. Briggs declared in the New York *Times* that these Christians "represent the most vigorous, burgeoning force in American religion today."

In such a time we are impelled to reflect on the purposes of God, who sends his Spirit where and when he wills. What is the meaning of the charismatic revival? Some are suggesting an apocalyptic explanation: the Rapture is just around the corner and soon thereafter the wrath of God will fall upon the wicked. As John Wesley White says in *WW III: Signs of the Impending Battle of Armageddon*, "The coming of Christ is to be preceded by another great outpouring of His Spirit" (p. 152).

My own study of Jesus' ministry and message leads to a different conclusion. I am convinced that God is calling us in the Spirit to give ourselves to the task of the inverted kingdom. It was first announced in Jesus' synagogue sermon at Nazareth. A contribution pinpointing the historical background that I have often sensed in this passage recently became available in the form of an extended article by James A. Sanders. Before relating his contribution toward clarifying the shape and setting of the inversion Jesus announced, let me set the stage for the first-century spiritual revival.

I

There are significant parallels between Jesus' time and ours that help us grasp the significance of the Nazareth sermon. Jesus' ministry began in response to the outbreak of the prophetic Spirit through John the Baptist. The tremendous excitement aroused by John can only be comprehended when we recall that for at least four hundred years, mainline Judaism had been teaching that God no longer spoke through living prophets. Four long centuries stood behind the belief that the age of prophecy was past, and that the present age was that of the commandment. Some of the later psalms reflect this idea. Psalm 74:9 complains, "There is no longer any prophet; and there is none among us who knows how long." The present, in other words, was a time when God no longer sent his Spirit to mankind. He no longer communicated directly. He was available only "in the Book," the Torah, the inspired list of his commandments.

This dogma about the silence of prophecy, the mysterious quenching of the Spirit, appears to have originated after the death of the last literary prophets, Haggai, Zechariah, and Malachi, in the fourth century B.C. The power of the dogma is visible in the fact that prophetic books composed after this period were all written under assumed names. For instance, the Testament of the Twelve Patriarchs was placed in the mouth of persons who had lived fifteen hundred years earlier. The books of Enoch, written in the New Testament era, purportedly originated even farther back than that. Prophetic writings could not be accepted from current authors, for, as the Syrian Apocalypse of Baruch stated, "The prophets have lain down to sleep" (85:3).

This disappearance of the Spirit was explained by the sin of Israel. God was accessible in the present, it was believed, only through the "echo of his voice" found in Scripture. And so the yearning arose for the dreadful period of the absent Spirit to end. People hoped for the time when the Messiah would come, lift the siege of divine wrath, and pour out the prophetic and enlivening Spirit upon the nation once again. This hope of release from alienation was described by Joachim Jeremias in *The Proclamation of Jesus* as follows:

> The idea of the quenching of the spirit is an expression of the consciousness that the present time is alienated from God. Time without the spirit is time under judgment. God is silent. Only in the last days will the disastrous epoch of the absence of the spirit come to an end and the spirit return again. There is abundant evidence of the degree to which people longed for the coming of the spirit. (P. 82)

With this widespread yearning, it is no wonder that John's ministry, proclaiming that the one who would come after him would baptize with the Spirit, aroused such anticipation. The opening of Jesus' public ministry fits the expectation exactly. Having experienced the gift of the Spirit at the time of his baptism, Jesus began his public work as a charismatic prophet, healing and proclaiming a new message with a power unknown in that era. While lacking the scribal education to be a rabbi, Jesus spoke with a remarkable authority. To cite Jeremias again, "Jesus . . . was regarded as a charismatic rather than as a professional theologian" (p. 77).

It was as a charismatic prophet, therefore, that Jesus returned to his home synagogue with the declaration that broke the silence of four hundred years. He selected this reading from the Isaiah scroll: "The Spirit of the Lord is upon me, because he has anointed me to preach good news to the poor. He has sent me to proclaim release to the captives and recovering of sight to the blind, to set at liberty those who are oppressed, to proclaim the acceptable year of the Lord." Then he coolly added the earthshaking line, "Today this scripture has been fulfilled in your hearing."

In other words, the centuries of the quenched Spirit have ended—today! The long period of Israel's sin and alienation is over—today! The power of the prophetic word to reveal the secrets of the heart and chart a path through the tangle of current decisions is present—today! What a joyous word this should have been! What burdens of guilt and alienation it promised to lift! What hope it offered! And yet . . .

II

The response of the synagogue in Nazareth was one of sullen rage. We do not get a full account of this in Luke, but the ensuing debate between Jesus and his former neighbors, and the fact that they tried to lynch him after the sermon, reveal the problem. The religious leaders of the synagogue were appalled because Jesus said nothing about God's wrath against the wicked as the means by which the kingdom would come. Not only had he failed to stress this widely accepted point, but he also deliberately cut short the Scripture reading to achieve his purpose. As scholars have often noticed, Jesus left off reading Isa. 61:2 in the very middle of the sentence. He omitted the line that followed "the acceptable year of the Lord." In the Isaiah scroll it reads: ". . . the acceptable year of the Lord *and a day of vengeance for our God.*" This unprecedented editing of the inspired text provides the context for the charge about Jesus being merely the "son of Joseph," which otherwise makes little sense. In effect they were complaining, as Jeremias puts it in *Jesus' Promise to the Nations:* "He has not studied, he is not ordained, how dare he presume to announce the coming of the messianic age, and by what right does he take upon himself to mutilate Holy Writ?" (P. 45.)

Jesus offended the Nazareth audience at two crucial points. He eliminated divine wrath against the enemies of

Israel, and he challenged the dogma of a totally inspired Scripture to accomplish this. When he said, "Today this scripture is fulfilled," he obviously meant the "acceptable year of the Lord" and not "a day of vengeance for our God." It was shocking. To put it in terms understandable for our time, Jesus did not adhere to the literal inspiration of Scripture. And as Jeremias insists, Jesus separated "the nationalistic idea of revenge from the hope of redemption" (p. 43). That is why it seems so strange for popular pamphlets like Stott's *The Authority of the Bible* to claim that "the overriding reason for accepting the divine inspiration and authority of Scripture is plain loyalty to Jesus" (p. 7). It cannot be loyalty to the Jesus who preached the Nazareth sermon. Despite the perplexities it causes for modern Fundamentalism, the fact remains that the first mortal danger Jesus faced in his ministry resulted from his opposition to the vengeance tradition, which led him to act in practical violation of the dogma of literal inspiration prevalent in his time.

From the perspective of the citizens of Nazareth, John the Baptist's message was greatly preferable to this. They would have applauded the idea that "even now the axe is laid to the root of the trees" (Matt. 3:10). They wanted the messianic age to come with violence against the wicked. The Romans, the Syrians, the Sidonians and the Greeks who polluted the Promised Land, who exploited and oppressed the innocent, should be annihilated! The Messiah would surely be the one who, in John's words, "will purge his threshing floor and gather his wheat into the granary, but the chaff he will burn with unquenchable fire" (Matt. 3:12).

The preference of the Nazareth congregation for the violent form of redemption was grounded in a major strand of Old Testament religion. For example, Psalm 37 says:

> But the wicked perish;
> the enemies of the Lord are like
> the glory of the pastures,
> they vanish—like smoke they vanish away.

> Mark the blameless man, and behold the upright,
>   for there is posterity for the man of peace.
> But transgressors shall be altogether destroyed;
>   the posterity of the wicked shall be cut off.
>   (Ps. 37:20, 37-38)

Jesus' townspeople believed, of course, that such wrath
would be directed primarily against their enemies in other
countries, against pagans who did not share the Jewish faith.
One thinks of Rabbi Eliezer Ben Hyrcanus' statement cited
by Jeremias in *Jesus' Promise to the Nations:* "No Gentile will
have a part in the world to come" (p. 40). In other words,
even if there is a fairly good pagan once in a while, they are
all going to hell in the end. Other opinions were even more
ferocious. One of the first-century sayings cited in the Talmud was noted by Martin Hengel in *Victory Over Violence:*
"Whoever spills the blood of one of the godless is like one
who offers sacrifice" (p. 49). To put it in terms that we can
understand, killing an evildoer is as good as going to church!
Such convictions were explicitly linked by Jesus' generation
to the Isaiah passage, as a reference in the Dead Sea Scrolls
makes plain. The members of the Qumran community were
enjoined to maintain "eternal hatred toward all men of perdi-
tion," but to keep it quiet until the messianic age had dawned.
When the moment to strike arrived, the prescription was that
"everyone is to be zealous for the law and in his day for the
day of vengeance." (I QS 9:21f.) The holy war would accomplish all that Isa. 61:2 seemed to promise.

So the people in Jesus' audience, reared with a religion
fiercely devoted to absolute justice, and believing that evil
must be destroyed for good to prevail, were enraged. And I
think we should be able to comprehend their rage. Present-
day Americans may not read the bloodier psalms too frequently and they may not dwell on the wrathful side of the
Old Testament prophets. Yet every evening on television we
witness and applaud the vengeance wreaked against "bad
guys." Evildoers are pictured as aggressively attacking the
innocent and flouting the law. Usually the normal agencies

of law enforcement prove powerless to cope with such threats, so a superhuman hero or heroine must arise to face wickedness for the sake of the community. In a dramatic fight scene the superhero or heroine always prevails against the foe, thus redeeming the community in the nick of time. This kind of story has dominated popular entertainments in America since the 1930's; it is a powerful and persuasive restatement of the redemption drama favored in the Nazareth synagogue. What disguises the similarity in part is the lack of explicitly religious terminology and the preference for selfless, even-tempered heroes. Starsky and Hutch come across as cool avengers, more attractive to current taste than the angry zealots of Old Testament religion, but the crooks who fall in that final moment of gunfire are just as dead. And the audience gains a kind of quiet satisfaction that justice always prevails at the end of these popular melodramas. The superheroes in current entertainment play the messianic role of bringing the kingdom, so to speak. They relieve the community from the threat of evil by means of selfless violence. Recent studies indicate that by the time the average American reaches his sixteenth birthday, he will have witnessed some 18,000 killings on television. About half of those killed will be the victims of the bad guys, and the other half will be the bad guys themselves, whose deaths are depicted as fully deserved.

The rationale of this current American version of the Nazareth yearning for a "day of vengeance for our God" was caught in several of the *All in the Family* episodes analyzed by Spencer Marsh in his witty book, *God, Man and Archie Bunker.* In an ironic way the producers of this television program allow Mike, the mustachioed young son-in-law, to state the view that Jesus was upholding in the synagogue. Archie of course maintains the traditional view. At one point Mike says, "Violence won't help," and Archie replies: "What's wrong with revenge? That's a perfect way to get even!" (P. 17.) In another episode Mike comes off as an atheist, the kind of heathen the Jews in Nazareth believed ought to be wiped out by God. Mike expounds that "there

is no heaven, there is no hell, and there is no God." Archie
is appalled, and when his antagonist begins to choke on his
dinner, Archie tells Gloria to stop pounding Mike on the
back so he can breathe.

> "That's God paying him back," Archie yells. "Serves you right,
> Meathead! Nobody fools around with the Lord. . . . Go get him,
> God! Give it to him good, God! Do your stuff, Lord." (P. 46)

III

This is the kind of tradition Jesus sought to invert in his
ministry. James A. Sanders shows, in his study of the interpretation of Isaiah 61 in the ancient period, that Jesus re-
versed the assumption of the Qumran community that the
"acceptable year of the Lord" would favor them. One of their
writings assumes that "the captives to be released are the
in-group, or Essenes." But "Jesus' citation of the gracious
acts of Elijah and Elisha toward the Sidonian widow and the
Syrian leper shows that he does not subscribe to the Essene
second axiom." The Essene interpretation had these axioms:
(1) the end time is present; (2) blessings are to be directed to
the Essene community and curses to all outsiders who do not
share the radical faith. Sanders goes on: "Jesus clearly shows
that the words meaning poor, captive, blind, and oppressed
do not apply exclusively to any in-group but, on the contrary,
apply to those whom God wishes them to apply. God sent
. . . Elijah and Elisha to outsiders, the Sidonian Widow and
the Syrian Leper." (P. 97.)

The theme of inverting favoritism is crucial for the verses
concerning where Jesus performed his miracles. He knew
precisely what was on the mind of his townspeople, that the
healings should have benefited them rather than their competitors in the next town. "Doubtless you will quote to me this
proverb, 'Physician, heal yourself [i.e., heal your own relatives
and neighbors first]; what we have heard you did at Capernaum, do here also in your own country.' " Jesus described the

fate of any prophet who is true to his calling of inverting the favored-nation assumption of his audience: "Truly, I say to you, no prophet is acceptable in his own country." (Luke 4:23f.) Sanders argues that the Lukan wording of this proverb, using "acceptable" rather than "not without honor" as in Matthew and Mark, is true to the original setting because it repeats the final word of the Isaiah citation. "No prophet, that is, no true prophet of the Elijah, Amos, Isaiah, Jeremiah type is *dektos* (acceptable) by his own countrymen precisely because his message always must bear in it a divine challenge to Israel's covenantal self-understanding in any generation." A true prophet "must cast a light of scrutiny upon his own people from the very source of authority on which they rely for their identity, existence and self-understanding." (P. 99.) Inversion is crucial to genuine prophecy. If a prophet is acceptable to his audience, confirming their feelings of superiority and their conviction of being God's favorites, he stands in the tradition of the false prophets.

One of the most serious failures of the New Apocalypticism is a lack of prophetic inversion. David Wilkerson relates in *The Vision* the five calamities of economic depression, natural disasters, moral disorder, youthful rebellion, and persecution that an angry God will unleash on the earth before annihilating the wicked. But "along with the vision of the calamities," Wilkerson writes, "God gave me a very special message of hope for all true believers. . . . Child of God, you need no longer fear . . . there is a hiding place for believers." (Pp. 115–117.) John Wesley White, in *WW III: Signs of the Impending Battle of Armageddon,* describes some nineteen "signs" that the final struggle is about to occur in which the sinners will be eradicated, while the saints will be spared. "While most of the world awaits extermination, the believer awaits evacuation. . . . Only those who have believed on Him for salvation will rise to be with him." (P. 202.)

The appeal of this theology is cosmic favoritism. It maintains the essential innocence and safety of ourselves while calling down destruction upon competitors in the next church, the next town, the alien country. These books are

modern embodiments of the Nazareth pique that the divine
will had strangely chosen to reveal itself first in Capernaum.
Despite their use of traditional Christian language, these
authors seem as far from the spirit of the Nazareth sermon
as were Jesus' original listeners. The fact that they make
themselves so "acceptable" in their own country, among the
audiences desiring reinforcement of a preferred status in the
eyes of God, reveals that they do not really stand in the
tradition of prophetic inversion. One of the most stunning
statements I discovered while reading the works of the New
Apocalypticism flatly repudiates the entire strand of prophetic inversion. In *Racing Toward Judgment,* David Wilkerson offers the "truest test of all" to determine the authenticity of a prophetic message: "True prophecy predicts doom for
the sinner and deliverance for the saints. Gloom to the children of this world, glory to the children of Heaven!" (Pp.
109f.) The folks at Nazareth could not have stated it more
clearly.

IV

Jesus' message to the Nazareth synagogue—and to all of
us—counters the entire tradition of divine favoritism. The
inverted kingdom invites the abandonment of the most-
favored-nation status because God is doing the unexpected.
The first are now last and the last first! God's mercy is extended to the outcasts, to all who consider themselves his
enemies. It is not reserved for the pious. In fact, to the extent
the pious feel they have a corner on God's love, they are cast
out and become "the last." In the measure that the wise and
sophisticated believe they alone have access to the depths of
grace, they lose the capacity to receive it and be transformed
by it. Divine love is unconditional, Jesus proclaimed. It is
impartial. "For he makes his sun rise on the evil and on the
good, and sends rain on the just and on the unjust" (Matt.
5:45).

This inversion theme is also implicit in the passage Jesus

read from Isaiah in the Nazareth synagogue. The proclamation of good news to the poor, healing for the sick, release to those held captive by insanity, and so forth, all sounds so positive and reasonable that the shocking inversion may not be visible. We need to recall the belief in the ancient period, a belief that has its parallels in modern American thought, that if you are poor, you probably deserve it. Poverty is a sign that you have sinned, that you have not worked hard enough, and that God does not smile on you. If you are afflicted with blindness, this must have been caused by Satan, or as a punishment for your sin. So you deserve your punishment! If you are in debtors' prison, you are suffering the just penalty for your sloth, your irresponsibility, and your sins. The final solution to most of these problems according to the Nazareth religion was the threshing sledge, the ax, and the fire. Waste them! Cleanse the Holy Land of all defilements! Let no cripple or diseased person stand before God's Temple or in his kingdom! Let Israel be reduced to a righteous, healthy remnant, and then the kingdom will surely be present!

The sermon in Nazareth inverted this entire tradition, because the unconditional love of God eliminates the need for such violent social solutions—whether performed against freaks on the television screen, in the death camps of the Nazi era, or on the street corners of the first century. Moreover, if God loves impartially, the deep psychological need to blame others is overcome. If I am not being blamed, there is no longer any need for me to accuse others or punish them. If I am not being accepted on the basis of my accomplishments, there is no necessity to envy the seemingly superior status of others, or to feel superior to those who have not been as fortunate as I.

The centrality of the inversion tneme is visible in the examples Jesus selected from the Old Testament to answer the angry objections of the synagogue. As Luke reports it, Jesus referred to I Kings 17, where the prophet Elijah was sent to Zarephath in Sidon to raise and heal the son of a foreign woman. Sidon was in enemy territory, formerly Phoenicia, now a part of war-torn Lebanon. It was the region from which the wicked Queen Jezebel had originated. Zarephath was therefore associated with the perverse religion and politics of the prophets of Baal, against whom Elijah was struggling so passionately. Yet when the famine was on, the prophet gave aid to none of the chosen people, but only to this outsider from the land of God's supposed enemies. This may well have been the only episode in the life of Elijah that fit Jesus' conviction about the thrust of the kingdom, because most of that prophet's career was devoted to a holy war against Baalism. Yet there it stood within the Scripture which the Nazareth townspeople felt was inspired: a counter example pointing beyond the entire violent tradition to a more humane alternative.

This incredible inversion was equaled in the second incident Jesus cited. Naaman the leper was an officer of an enemy army. He was fighting for Syria, with its capital at Damascus, the most hated of Israel's ancient enemies. Even today there is no nation more despicable in Jewish eyes than Syria. Yet II Kings 5 reports the dramatic story to which Jesus referred, in which the haughty officer was impelled to wash himself in the Jordan River to be healed from his affliction. Although Jesus does not specifically refer to it, Naaman too had to give up his feeling of superiority. His angry response to the command to bathe seven times in the Jordan would probably have been vividly recalled by Jesus' audience: "Behold, I thought that he [Elisha] would surely come out to me, and stand, and call on the name of the LORD his God, and wave his hand over the place, and cure the leper. Are not Abana and Pharpar, the rivers of Damascus, better than all the waters of Israel? Could I not wash in them, and be clean? So he turned and went away in a rage" (II Kings 5:11–12).

So when you think about it, the inversion is complete: each nation and person harboring illusions of superiority must give them up. The rivers of Damascus are not intrinsically superior in God's eyes, nor are the rivers of Israel, or America, or Russia, or Japan. For genuine healing to occur, Naaman had to submit to the waters of the enemy people; the Nazareth audience in turn had to admit that God sent Elisha to none but this enemy officer. In a reversal of much that the violent prophet stood for, his errand of mercy to the hateful and arrogant pagan provided a paradigm for the age of the Spirit.

At the root of each episode that Jesus cited stands the powerful love of God that comes to friend and foe alike. God is not the tyrant who loves only those who obey him, who hates those who oppose his law. He is the Abba who loves each of his wayward children unconditionally, seeking the best for them, and working to counter the prejudices that divide them from one another. This powerful divine love turns nationalistic biases upside down and inverts the preference every chosen group thinks it deserves. The message of the inverted kingdom is that the dynamic love of the Father equalizes all of his children, of every race and color and political persuasion. Even his worst enemies can be recipients of that love, if they will only unbend their pride and accept it. Even the enemies in the Nazareth synagogue! Even the devotees of the New Apocalypticism! And even those who find themselves replying critically to the predictions about the end-time catastrophes that will somehow spare the innocent.

V

The theme of a great inversion plays a decisive role in Flannery O'Connor's powerful piece of Christian fiction, "Everything That Rises Must Converge." In this story, Julian Chestny is an educated Southerner, shaped by the civil rights advances of the 1950's and 1960's. He is trained to be a writer, but he subsists with his widowed mother as an unsuccessful typewriter salesman. Her insistence on maintaining the superior attitude of the plantation class, from which the family had descended through changing economic conditions, infuriates Julian. As mother and son make their way to the bus from a seedy apartment in a once elegant portion of the city, Mrs. Chestny comments on the low social status of the participants in the reducing class she is to attend. "Most of them in it are not our kind of people," she said, "but I can be gracious to anybody. I know who I am." Julian replies with the petulant certainty of the liberal who knows times have changed. An inversion has transpired to turn superior and inferior classes and identities upside down. "Knowing who you are is good for one generation only," Julian snaps. "You haven't the foggiest idea where you stand now or who you are." (P. 6.)

This statement proves prophetic as they encounter a huge, bristling black woman with a cute little boy on the bus to the Y. Julian had chosen to leave his seat next to his mother in order to join a black man on the opposite side of the aisle, aiming at embarrassing her with a demonstration of liberalism. But he is irritated when the black woman crowds into the seat while her child sits down with Mrs. Chestny. He takes grim delight at seeing that both women have on identical hats. When the black man rises at the next stop, the matron angrily snatches her child from the seat next to Mrs. Chestny. But the boy is soon able to slip out of her massive hands to rejoin his new white friend. " 'I think he likes me,' Julian's mother said, and smiled at the black woman. It was the smile she used when she was being particularly gracious to an inferior." They all get off at the next stop, and Julian has a sinking feeling when his mother reaches into her purse for a pickaninny's coin. " 'Don't do it!' Julian says fiercely between his teeth," but she cheerfully offers a bright new penny to the black child. (P. 20.)

An angry fist and bulging red pocketbook strike Mrs. Chestny to the sidewalk. "He don't take nobody's pennies!" shouted the black matron while disappearing down the street. Mrs. Chestny's heart condition cannot take the shock of this reversal on top of the contempt of her son. She collapses in a fatal heap while Julian frantically pounds off down the street for help.

"Everything That Rises Must Converge" articulates the issues and themes we must examine in following the implications of Jesus' message about the great inversion. Mrs.

Chestny comments on the new assertiveness of the American counterparts to the Syrian officer and Sidonite widow: "They should rise, yes, but on their own side of the fence" (p. 7). Yet she finds her fate determined by whether she can adapt to the new circumstances on the bus, and her dying thoughts are of her white grandpa and her black nurse, Caroline. Everything that rises must converge, so if the road from inversion does not lead to communion in life, it will inevitably lead to a communion in death. The historical Jesus saw this for his own doomed generation.

Our task in this era of the New Apocalypticism is to follow the Spirit's trajectory from its launching pad of the great inversion. We discover that it penetrates and explodes the "mental bubble" that each of us, like Julian Chestny, tends to erect around his theology and our view of reality. Julian loved to withdraw "into the inner compartment of his mind . . . when he could not bear to be part of what was going on around him. From it he could see out and judge but in it he was safe from any kind of penetration from without. It was the only place where he felt free from the general idiocy of his fellows." (P. 11.)

The Spirit has a way of bursting such judgmental bubbles so that persons and generations have a chance to face their responsibilities without illusions. But the aim of the puncture is to drive us out onto the path of the great inversion itself. The will of the Spirit manifesting itself in the current revival is implicit in the Nazareth sermon. Christians are to pass on the inversion in the form of the unconditional love of God wherever strife and illusions are habitual. In times of hatred and cynicism, the great inversion of Christ leads us to love the unlovable, to seek the release of captives wherever they are in the world, and to lift up the downtrodden and confused. When the world and the perverse impulses within our own hearts seek to hinder this mission, it is the Spirit that turns us around to walk back against the crowd as Jesus did at the brow of a Nazarene hill. The cross may loom on a distant height. But in the meanwhile, there is a path to follow —from the great inversion to the messianic feast.

Chapter IV

Except
the Sign
of Jonah

Matthew 16:1–4

There is an image like the sign of Jonah in the opening scene of John Cheever's novel, *Falconer.* After being sentenced for killing his brother, Farragut is being brought to Falconer Prison. Two contrasting images mark his entrance into captivity, the escutcheon above the main entrance and the blue sky. The stone emblem represented "Liberty, Justice and, between the two, the sovereign power of government." These were the stern realities that condemned him to what he feared would be a living death. The free, blue sky somehow symbolized the miracle of redemption from everything the escutcheon represented. The prison van stopped. "Farragut got to his feet. He saw the escutcheon for the first and, he thought, the last time. This was where he would die. Then he saw the blue sky and nailed his identity to it." (P. 5.) A patch of blue may seem too fragile to sustain the hope of freedom, yet it proves sufficient as Farragut discovers redemption in his confinement, and ultimately escapes because of the death of a friend. It is a kind of secular "sign of Jonah," an indication that even in the most wretched of times, redemption is a reality.

On several occasions Jesus was asked about the signs that might sustain the hope of freedom. Matthew 16:1–4 provides the account of one such occasion, in which the Pharisees and Sadducees "asked him to show them a sign from heaven." It was the central question of the age for a people obsessed with apocalyptic signs that might indicate the dawn of the messianic times, the date of the final warfare against Rome and its demonic allies, and the fierce blue hope of a millennial age of peace. His answer was most curious. In fact, it differs so widely from the books currently being written on the subject that they never seem to cite it at all. Jesus replied, "An evil and adulterous generation seeks for a sign, but no sign shall be given to it except the sign of Jonah" (Matt. 16:4). This poses several questions, which we shall attempt to answer: What did Jesus mean by this curious statement? What was his approach to the signs of the times? And what did he mean by "the sign of Jonah"?

I

"No sign shall be given. . . ." This stark repudiation of sign-giving is reported by each of the three Synoptic Gospels. Mark, the earliest written, provides the most pointed formulation: "Truly, I say to you, no sign shall be given to this generation" (Mark 8:12). Matthew 12:39 has another version of this negative statement that is almost word for word the same as in Matt. 16:4: "An evil and adulterous generation seeks for a sign; but no sign shall be given to it except the sign of the prophet Jonah." Luke provides a more elaborate statement of the Jonah theme, but retains the negative: "This generation . . . seeks a sign, but no sign shall be given to it except the sign of Jonah" (Luke 11:29). We shall take up the Jonah question in a moment, relating it to the amazing power of the gospel to convert murderers like the Ninevites, but first we need to understand the strange negative.

The contrast between Jesus' repudiation of sign-hunting and the popular religion of his time is striking and significant. We know how deeply the first-century counterparts of the New Apocalypticists were involved in calculating and peering for signs of the messianic era. Each time Jesus was asked to prove his messianic status by "signs," his audience expected detailed references about the planets or the calendar, the prediction of earthquakes and storms, or some other miraculous indication that the end times had arrived. Many of the writings found at Qumran, the so-called Dead Sea Scrolls, are full of this sort of material. The most popular religious books and pamphlets of Jesus' day were rife with speculations about when the Old Testament prophecies of Ezekiel, Daniel, and Zechariah were to be fulfilled and how they correlated with current events. The calendrical and astrological speculations in writings like The Book of Jubilees aimed at the same end, giving the faithful a schedule of the signs of the times so that they could distinguish the significant from the trivial. These first-century efforts were more complicated and serious than most of our modern efforts. They also proved about as wrong in the end.

Jesus rejected all of this. Consequently, the first point we need to get straight as we look through the books of the New Apocalypticism is Jesus' own unequivocal word: "No sign shall be given . . . except the sign of Jonah."

This is difficult to accept when so much of the New Testament itself does not conform to Jesus' radical view. There is a long discussion about the signs of the times in Mark 13 and its parallels; I and II Thessalonians treat such matters at length; and the book of Revelation is as full of such speculation as anything in the Dead Sea Scrolls. Many of these statements about the signs of the times and the schedule of the apocalyptic warfare are placed in the mouth of Jesus by the writers of the New Testament. Scholars have had a difficult job of sorting to do. But we cannot settle the issue as the devotees of the New Apocalypticism would like to, by ignoring the key passages in which Jesus refused to provide signs to his first-century audience. We must honestly confront the fact that when the most widely accepted standards for ascertaining an authentic saying of Jesus are applied, this radical refusal looks original; much of the other material looks like imitations of traditional apocalypses.

One criterion for authenticity, as Norman Perrin has defined it, is "multiple attestation." Is the saying found in more than one strand of the synoptic material? The "sign of

Jonah" saying passes this test because it is reflected in each of the Gospels, and in the sayings source that scholars call Q. A more crucial criterion is "dissimilarity." Is the saying different from the traditions current in the ancient period? The more original a saying appears to be, the higher its claim to authenticity. In this regard, the no-sign statement in Matthew 16 differs from what the various branches of the Jewish community taught; it differs from the views of the early church, and also from those of the Gospel writers themselves. The "sign of Jonah" saying could therefore hardly have been transferred to Jesus from the beliefs of the early church, or slipped into the tradition from Judaism. Its originality points directly to the genius of the historical Jesus. A third criterion is "coherence." Are there close and logical connections with other authentic sayings? As we shall see, the unexpected prophecy in Matt. 16:1–4 ("No sign shall be given") is certainly congruent with other key passages that appear to have solid claims to authenticity.

The point is worth belaboring because we need a firm basis for what is to follow. Jesus disliked the kind of sign-searching his generation was doing. And his attitude pertains every bit as much to current enthusiasts who persistently claim to be following Jesus in their elaborate discussions of the signs. In fact, they have overlooked his unique and fundamental premise.

II

The crucial question is, Why? Why did Jesus refuse to provide signs? The reasons are revealed in the wording of his answer to the request. "An evil and adulterous generation seeks a sign," Matthew reports. "You hypocrites!" is added by Luke, in 12:56. For some reason, Jesus connected the quest for signs with evil, with adultery, and with hypocrisy. This will require some explaining.

One of the features of the "signs of the times" is that they are usually thought to favor the chosen few. Read the current books about the signs pointing to the Rapture. How many of them assume that the author and his group will be part of the 144,000 saints to be saved at the last minute before the conflagration of the planet? Or, in the case of those who believe the number of those raptured will far exceed this reference from the book of Revelation, how frequently is the assumption made that the "saints" who agree with the New Apocalypticism will be included? All of the books I have examined imply such claims. When the social trends are cited as signs of the end time, how often does one read references to trends an author favors? Not often. For the most part, it is the triumph of forces he detests, the development of trends he hates, or the victory at the polls of a party he distrusts that are the "signs" of the impending end. The same generalization can be made about the apocalyptic writings produced by the Essenes and other groups in Jesus' time.

This connects with Jesus' charge about the "evil and adulterous generation" that seeks signs. Such a generation is adulterous in the sense of lacking covenant loyalty to God whose ways are not our ways, and who is not partial to our narrow interests. The underlying loyalty in sign-seeking is to oneself and to one's group, not to the transcendent Creator who refuses to be idolized or to dwell in houses and definitions made by humankind. Seeking signs is a matter of refusing to allow God to control the future as he wills. In practice, it presumes to measure the divine will according to limited human standards such as whether a trend suits me, or whether the time is ripe for my group to come out on top. Sign-seeking is the human effort to manipulate God's open future, to penetrate the silence he imposes, and to exploit such knowledge for rather narrow purposes. Such behavior is "evil" in the sense that it produces grim results in history: wars, brutality, hardness of heart, delight in the suffering of others, and passivity in the face of adverse circumstances.

In a closely related line of thought, Luke reports that Jesus connected the quest for signs with "hypocrisy," which is piety disguising self-interest. This insight may be hard to take, but the insight probes to the center of the sore. On the surface, books dealing with the signs of the times appear to be pious. They are full of Scripture citations and often contain evangelical material of real substance. But underneath, it is the future of the chosen people, the in-group, which stands at the center. Take the first-century apocalyptic writings as an example. For the most part, they aimed to discover the proper moment to revolt against Rome so that divine favor would assist the pious in gaining superior status in the world. The authors of these writings cared not a whit for the suffering of innocent foreigners in the disasters they predicted, in the earthquakes, hailstorms, and conflagrations for which they yearned. The aim was to confirm the superiority of the chosen people, to give them advantages at the expense of others. Yet all of this selfish cruelty, so much at variance with the best of Hebraic religion, was covered with a pious veneer of honestly awaiting God's signs, humbly looking for the fulfillment of his promises. Despite the obvious sincerity of apocalyptic devotees then and now, sign-seeking was and is, as Jesus stated so bluntly, *hypocrisy.*

III

Once we understand this radical insight of Jesus, we are prepared to grasp his remarkable comments concerning the need for common sense in interpreting history. According to Matthew 16, Jesus' immediate response to the request for a sign was a discussion about the weather. He came from farming country, and knew how much his people in Galilee—like those of us from similar regions today—looked for rain clouds and sunsets. I have lived most of my life in areas where the weather report is the most important news of the day. To me, Jesus' words appear on the surface to make perfect sense. "When it is evening, you say, 'It will be fair weather; for the sky is red.' And in the morning, 'It will be stormy today, for the sky is red and threatening.' You know how to interpret the appearance of the sky, but you cannot interpret the signs of the times" (Matt. 16:2–3).

This is all so reasonable and familiar that the question must be jarred loose from our minds. What is it that hinders human beings from being as practical, as commonsensical, about the signs of the times as they are about the weather? On the basis of Jesus' opening remarks, the answer is obvious. Self-interest is what impairs our judgment about history. The yearning for superior status is what leads us to accept only those signs that point to our side's triumph. Our hatred for adversaries, and the desire to see the wicked suffer, are what keep us from acknowledging any signs in their favor. In short, it is the wicked, adulterous, and hypocritical tendencies of the heart that keep humankind from being as sensible about history as we are about the weather.

But that is not all. Given this perversity, as characteristic of our time as of theirs, the most routine and predictable thing one could say about the signs of the times is that those who claim to interpret them are inevitably wrong. There is a regularity in the failure of such predictions that can be compared with the red sky in Palestine, where the rains always came from the west and the dry winds from the east. Let us review this history of failed predictions for a moment, calling to mind what Jesus' conversation partners would have remembered about the recent past.

In 4 B.C., a little over thirty years before the conversation reported by Matthew, three messianic figures arose to proclaim that the signs of the times pointed to the Last Judgment and the restoration of Israel's glory. The sign itself was apparently the death of Herod the Great, for Simon, Athronges, and Judas the Galilean all started their rebellions simultaneously when Herod's death was reported. Thousands of faithful Zealots joined them. The Roman legionnaires put down the rebellions with relentless fury. They crucified two thousand of the rebels on the roads around Jerusalem as an example. In places like Sepphoris, a town three miles north of Nazareth, all of the citizens were sold into slavery for participating in the rebellion. The intervention of the heavenly host, predicted by the rebels according to Old Testament sayings, failed to take place.

Ten years later, in A.D. 6, at the time of the census in Judea, outbreaks occurred again. An organized guerrilla movement led by Judas the Galilean and Zadok the Pharisee began to operate against the Romans. They taught that zealous violence would itself be a sign, a way of impelling God to intervene. According to Martin Hengel's reconstruction of the Zealot movement, the resistance of these men and their successors continued through the time of Jesus, with scattered incidents of ambush and assassination of collaborators. Barabbas, whom the Jews demanded in place of Jesus at the time of his crucifixion, was probably one of these freedom fighters, which explains his popularity with the crowd. Despite his unusual release, the end of such rebellions large and small was as predictable and as red as the Judean sunset.

But the story does not end there. The obsession about signs gathered momentum in the decades after Jesus uttered his stark warning. In the mid-40's of the first century, according to Hengel's *Victory Over Violence,* there were vigorous Roman campaigns against the "robber bands" in Judea, which were probably Zealot in their orientation (pp. 32ff.). By the late 50's, lynching of collaborators by these Zealot groups became widespread, and in the early 60's the apocalyptic fanaticism invaded urban areas, dividing Jerusalem into camps controlled by rival gangs. The obsessive commitment to in-group concerns, a central motivation in apocalyptic thought, split society into feuding factions, some vying for influence with a corrupt Roman administration, and each prepared to commit any crime to achieve its holy cause.

When the Jewish-Roman war broke out in A.D. 66, this vicious apocalyptic factionalism emerged with predictably disastrous consequences. Rival revolutionary groups struggled for domination, with armed conflict between them beginning the moment the Romans were driven out. Josephus refers to the "false prophets," "impostors," and "deceivers" who impelled these factions to their incredible excesses of brutality. David M. Rhoads's study, *Israel in Revolution,* shows that Josephus thoroughly disapproved of their apocalyptic fanaticism, which explains the derogatory terms he

employed in describing their activities (p. 163). It is clear that
sign-seeking was producing its predictable harvest. As Martin Hengel observes: "The effect of such 'prophecies' upon
the unsophisticated can hardly be over-estimated" (p. 39).
There were over a million casualties in this awful war, and
the expectation of divine intervention persisted right up to
the bloody end. To quote Hengel again: "Even when the
capture of the sanctuary (of the temple) by the Romans was
imminent, a Zealot prophesied that God was about to reveal
a 'sign of his redemption' in the sanctuary, inducing thousands to go up to the temple, where they were then cut down
by the invading Romans" (p. 39). Finally, in A.D. 73, the last
of the Zealots who were holding out on the mountain strong-
hold of Masada after the fall of Jerusalem gave up on the
signs when the Roman dike and battering rams had reached
the height of their fortifications. They committed mass suicide to ensure that their wives and children would not go into
the degradation of a Roman captivity.

One of the things that a study of sign-seeking reveals is
that disappointments do not quench the yearning for certainty. Despite the terrible sufferings of the Jewish-Roman
war, apocalyptic visions did not vanish. In A.D. 132–135, the
Bar Cochba revolt occurred in the same territory, for virtually the same reasons, and with the same expectations. The
messianic figure Bar Cochba, son of the light, was himself
presumably the sign that this time God would intervene. God
did not. Thousands were again killed; Jerusalem was leveled
and then turned into a pagan city. Archaeologists have recently found the remains of Bar Cochba's followers and their
families where they fled to caves after the destruction of their
hopes. They died of thirst or suffocation after being cornered
by the Romans who built bonfires at the mouths of the caves,
if Yigael Yadin's account of the evidence is correct.

One could go on to trace the history of sign-seeking in the
centuries that followed. Scarcely a generation passed without
fanatics somewhere in the Jewish or Christian world rising
to proclaim the signs of the end. A great wave of such predictions occurred around the year 1000, for example. Then Joa-

chim of Fiore developed his modern-sounding apocalyptic vision, based on the book of Revelation, arguing that the millennial age would dawn sometime between 1200 and 1260. He died before this period had lapsed, but his followers attached their hopes to the son of Barbarossa, who was crowned emperor in 1220. He came to view himself as a kind of God incarnate. Even after his death, rumors and legends multiplied that he was returning to usher in the kingdom. As the year 1260 approached, groups of flagellants arose to proclaim that their self-inflicted wounds and journeys of penance had redemptive power. The Heavenly Letter that they believed they had received in 1260 gave them a consciousness of superiority similar to that of the Zealots of earlier Jewish history. These groups developed an extreme intolerance. Wherever they would travel in the Low Countries, they would drown or burn all the Jews they found in order to please God. Norman Cohn's *The Pursuit of the Millennium* traces the development of the flagellant groups, pointing out how the disappointment of the hopes concerning the year 1260 did little to dampen their enthusiasm (pp. 124ff.). One of the figures who won popular support as a resurrected Frederick was Konrad Schmid. He forecast that the Last Judgment and the millennium would start in 1369, but was burned as a heretic the year before his prophecy failed.

In the first half of the fifteenth century, Bohemia became a center of apocalyptic enthusiasm. A group of reforming factions called the "Taborites" decided that the signs of the times indicated that the middle of February, in the year 1420, would be the date when God would destroy every wicked city in Christendom except their five strongholds. When the world remained intact in the later days of the month, the apocalyptic enthusiasm did not subside. Under the pressure of political opposition and the threat of persecution, the Taborites decided they should massacre everyone who did not subscribe to their views. Their preachers proclaimed: "Accursed be the man who withholds his sword from shedding the blood of the enemies of Christ. Every believer must wash his hands in that blood." Cohn notes that the brutalities evoked by such zealous commands brought a terrible retribution when the Taborites were annihilated in the subsequent siege (pp. 224f.).

A century later the Peasants' Revolt broke out in Germany, stimulated in part by Thomas Münzer's claim to have seen signs in the heavens that God would intervene on the side of the oppressed farmers. His army of peasants armed with scythes and sticks were slaughtered by the armored knights, while Münzer maintained to the end that God would send his heavenly army and that he himself could catch enemy cannonballs in his sleeves. He was captured, tortured, drawn and quartered on May 27, 1525, the very year he had predicted for the end of the world.

It would perhaps be tedious to recount all the activities and campaigns of the Puritans, many of them following signs of divine favor, but ultimately ending in the defeat of Cromwell and the transfer of his virulent legacy to America. One thinks of the dozens of times during British and American history when predictions about the end of the world have been made. Ernest R. Sandeen provides many of these details in *The Roots of Fundamentalism*. The identification of the revolutionary events in the 1790's with the prophecies in Daniel 7 and Revelation 13 "provided biblical commentators with a prophetic Rosetta stone" to calculate the signs of the end (p. 7). A number of groups used these details to predict the millennium in the 1830's. Thereafter figures like Michael Baxter set about the task of discovering what went wrong in the calculations. He "managed to predict incorrect dates from 1861 through 1908, presumably being saved only by death from an infinite series" (p. 59).

In a different cultural setting, but the same time period, a Mennonite preacher by the name of Claass Epp decided that the schedule of Daniel and Revelation meant the Rapture would occur on March 8, 1889. Fred Richard Belk's *The Great Trek* tells the remarkable story of the resultant migration of colonists to Turkestan, the one area that would presumably not be destroyed in the tribulation. When the appointed day arrived, the prophet Epp sat on a "throne" of a church altar table, surrounded by the white-robed community, waiting for the Rapture that never came. The village survived until 1935 when the Soviets forcibly removed Epp's descendants for refusing to participate in the collectivization plan.

Dwight Wilson's study, *Armageddon Now! The Premillenarian Response to Russia and Israel Since 1917,* describes the outbursts of excitement among American fundamentalists starting in the year when Jerusalem was captured from the Turks. The end of the world was thought to be imminent because the Jews could now reestablish themselves in the Holy City. In an article by a Christian and Missionary Alliance writer, Wilson found this announcement: "How stupendous the significance of this event must be is impossible for the most intense language to exaggerate. . . . An age-long period of more than twenty-five centuries is closing . . . and we are already in the beginning of the end." The following year *The Weekly Evangel* stated that "all schools of interpretation" were agreed that the freeing of Jerusalem took place on schedule and that the end would come in 1934 (p. 44). All through the 1920's, according to Wilson, the anticipation of Armageddon was intense. By 1939, events like the German-Soviet nonaggression pact were seen as the fulfillment of Ezekiel's prophecy and a prelude to the final battle, which many believed to be starting in the blitzkrieg of that year. In an Assembly of God editorial of Dec. 23, 1939, the faithful were told: "With the nations rushing on so swiftly to Armageddon the appearance of the Lord should be our constant expectation, for surely His coming draweth nigh" (p. 118). Wilson goes on to cite dozens of premillennialist editorials and speeches that proclaim the end-time events in virtually every political and military development down to the Yom Kippur war. He concludes:

> The current crisis was always identified as a sign of the end. . . . Speculation on the Antichrist has included Napoleon, Mussolini, Hitler, and Henry Kissinger. The northern confederation was supposedly formed by the Treaty of Brest-Litovsk, the

Rapallo Treaty, the Nazi-Soviet Pact, and then the Soviet Bloc.
. . . The end of the "times of the Gentiles" has been placed in
1895, 1917, 1948, and 1967. "Gog" has been an impending
threat since the Crimean War, both under the Czars and the
Communists. (P. 216)

Historian Wilson, a product of the premillennialist tradition,
anticipates that the end-time speculation will increase "as the
year 2000 approaches" because of the possibilities of iden-
tifying the third millennium as "the Thousand Year Kingdom of Christ" (p. 13).

The dynamics of such predictions and their failure were
explored by Leon Festinger and his colleagues in *When
Prophecy Fails*. Their detailed case history of an end-time
prediction indicates that disappointments about failure result
in increased evangelistic activity aimed at providing confirmation through conversion of others. Rather than being
discouraged, the true believers hold to the truth of their
convictions all the more firmly when the end does not come
on schedule. This is why a history of the Millerites should be
required reading for everyone committed to the New Apocalypticism. They were the predecessors of the Seventh Day
Adventists, first setting the date for the end of the world in
1843. Accounts of the Jehovah's Witnesses, the Mormons, or
the Black Muslims would serve the same purpose. In all these
episodes, some comical and some tragic, the one invariable
element is that God does not intervene on schedule. His
heavenly host is not activated by any of the signs. The por-
tents that promise to guarantee the turnabout in favor of
in-groups prove fickle.

Is it not of immediate importance, in view of such events,
to take up the cause of common sense that the historical Jesus
was recommending? Is it not time to acknowledge the bias
in our egocentric predictions? To admit the self-interest in
our confident assertions that the Late Great Planet Earth is
about to be destroyed so the saintly few can enjoy a peaceable
kingdom? Is the time not ripe for Christians to turn their
back on this kind of hypocrisy, this adulterous attempt to

manipulate God's future for our own ends? Is it not time, after two thousand years, to apply at least as much horse sense to the signs of the times as we do to the weather?

IV

All of this leaves us with—the sign of Jonah. "No sign will be given" to this evil and adulterous generation, said Jesus, "except the sign of Jonah." A great deal has been written to explain this saying, including a full-length book by Richard Alan Edwards with the title *The Sign of Jonah: In the Theology of the Evangelists and Q.* Without going into the complicated details, his thesis is that two of the parallel passages to our text reflect the thinking of the post-Easter community. He sees Jonah as a parallel figure to Jesus, the preacher of repentance who experienced three days in the belly of the earth as Jonah did in the belly of the whale. Edwards views the "sign of Jonah" saying in Matthew 16 as a composite of the other versions. This does not appear plausible. Given the coherence and originality of the oracle in Matthew, there is good reason to believe that it is the original and accurate version of the Jesus saying, and that the other Gospels provide efforts by early Christians to interpret the strange saying. In the context of Jesus' outlook, the "sign of Jonah" appears to be a reference to the power of the gospel to convert the worst of evildoers, represented by the citizens of Nineveh, the capital of hated Assyria in its heyday.

I believe that in the Jonah saying Jesus essentially gives the same answer that he gave to the disciples of John the Baptist as they asked him if he was the "one who was to come." He pointed to the crowd and said, "The blind receive their sight and the lame walk, lepers are cleansed and the deaf hear, and the dead are raised up, and the poor have good news preached to them" (Matt. 11:5). In other words, the program of Isaiah, which Jesus read in that first sermon at Nazareth, is being fulfilled. That is the sign of the presence of the kingdom of God. The gospel works! The "good news to the poor" mentioned in Isaiah 61 is powerful enough to redeem the irredeemable. God's love is sufficient to heal the hopeless and helpless. So the world does not have to be destroyed for the kingdom to come! God's will is not going to be accomplished by blasts and earthquakes, and certainly not by hailstones from heavenly helicopters directed against women and children of some enemy race. No, the sign of Jonah is the power of the gospel, which eliminates the very *raison d'être* of "signs of the times" in the traditional sense of the term.

This, of course, is what much of Jesus' audience did not want to hear. If the sign of Jonah is all one is going to receive, what happens to the yearning to be number one? To the hope of the annihilation of one's enemies? To the dream of a conflict-free world, in which the chosen people enjoy heavenly comforts while others burn in nuclear holocausts? The answer is obvious. The evil and adulterous heart and the hypocritical spirit lead us—like Jonah in the story—to wish that the gospel might fail. Jonah fled to Tarshish to get as far away as he possibly could from his mission to preach to Nineveh. He was aghast at the prospect that the gospel might work, that Nineveh would not be destroyed. When he was gently but firmly nudged in the direction of responsibilities by the great fish episode in this delightful short story at which Jesus must have chuckled many times, Jonah finally went to the enemy city to preach the word. And to his horror, the gospel worked. Even though his proclamation was less than enthusiastic, and his message eliminated the element of promise as much as possible, the Ninevites repented. By order of the emperor, not only the citizens but also the beasts of the field repented in sackcloth and ashes. "When God saw what they did, how they turned from their evil way, God repented of the evil which he had said he would do to them, and he did not do it" (Jonah 3:10).

There is always something incalculable about redemption, which is why all we can have is a sign pointing toward it. We cannot fathom the reality itself. How could the most wicked people on earth, not to speak of the dumb cattle of Assyria, have been transformed by Jonah's begrudged and mutilated proclamation? There are surely innumerable counter examples, in which even the most enlightened and inspired preaching falls on deaf ears. Redemption is a miracle, as even the literature of our own era affirms. In John Cheever's novel, *Falconer,* Farragut's friend Jody says as much in revealing his plan to escape from prison by joining the cardinal's altar attendants and departing from the special prison Mass on the helicopter: "When we land I'll get out of my robes in the vestry and walk out on the street. What a miracle!" (P. 98.)

Against all probabilities, Jody's plan works, and even the prison commissioner unknowingly bears witness to the sign of Jonah. In his talk before the Mass, he extols the cooperation of public agencies that led to the remarkable feat in the history of penal reform. Not only have eight prisoners graduated, but the cardinal has flown in for the celebration. They "have accomplished what we might compare—compare only, of course—to a miracle. These eight humble men have passed with honors a most difficult test that many well-known captains of industry have failed." (P. 129.) But the real miracle in Cheever's novel is that of redemption. Jody makes good his escape and even the cardinal lends some aid. Knowing full well where the cocky man in liturgical attire originated, he beckons Jody to a meeting in a store down the street in New York. Like the guest in Jesus' parable of the wedding banquet, he is transformed by a new set of clothes.

> Jody was measured with a tape. "You're built like a tailor's dummy," said the man. This went to Jody's head, but he definitely felt that vanity was out of place in the miracle. Twenty minutes later he walked up Madison Avenue. His walk was springy—the walk of a man going to first on balls, which can, under some circumstances, seem to be a miracle. (Pp. 132f.)

It was a miracle of redemption that even succeeded for a moment in burning away the pride from someone who had suffered from it all his life.

The larger miracle in John Cheever's modern sign of

Jonah relates to Farragut himself. In prison for a crime of
zeal, killing his hateful brother with a fire poker, Farragut
writes complaining letters to the authorities. He goes into a
destructive tantrum after being deprived of his methadone in
a typical instance of prison bumbling. But gradually he is
shaken out of his reveries and begins to live in the now. The
love of fellow inmates and the unannounced substitution of
placebos for his drug eliminate his dependency. He begins to
make plans for his own escape to freedom. The means of his
redemption are all problematic; the setting is unpromising in
the extreme, yet in the end, the supreme miracle occurs. A
degenerate college professor from a twisted family, who had
fallen prey to the most debasing habits of our age, was free.
The sign of Jonah, ironic and yet strangely joyous, had mani-
fested itself again.

V

So in the end, Jesus did not leave his audience—or us—
without any sign at all. He did not leave us directionless in
a vast and threatening universe. There is a sign, the sign of
Jonah, which we can recover through the study of the Judeo-
Christian tradition, and which we can see manifesting itself
in the revival of our day, despite all its problematic qualities.
The gospel about the love of God, expressed toward evil and
good alike in the life and death of Jesus the son of God, still
has the power to transform. It is still the clearest sign we have
that God is present and active in this battered world, still the
best clue we have as to what we should do with our lives and
with our history. But it is a sign that will not tolerate our
self-centered behavior; it will not leave our evil, our adultery,
or our hypocrisy untouched. For if we take the gospel seriously, and allow its power within our hearts, it can eliminate
the very impulse toward such perversities. What need have
we to manipulate the world in an adulterous fashion if God
loves us and cares for us through good and evil days alike?
What reason do we have for hypocrisy if God loves and

accepts us unconditionally, not judging us by appearances, but loving us as we are? What need is there for us to participate in the evil of sign-seeking if divine love promises to conduct us through the darkest future?

To let the gospel work on us is to overcome the prejudices and fears that close the mind. It is to allow common sense and prudent judgment to prevail. To live by this sign is to learn to laugh as the author of Jonah did at the silly, chauvinistic behavior of himself and his people, so certain that God preferred them over the Ninevites. It is to recognize our own image in Jonah's anger when the little gourd plant wilted over his head, after he had callously desired the death, the ultimate wilting, of thousands of Ninevites. If the sign of Jonah means the triumph of the gospel, even over Jonah himself, then each of us must base our lives on unconditional acceptance alone. When this is done, each will come to acknowledge that he is no better than others; each will come to a realistic sympathy for the plight of others; and each will see with clear-eyed realism what must be done to keep this planet intact. Wherever we may be in absorbing its implications, the word remains in both its judgment and its promise: "No sign shall be given . . . except the sign of Jonah."

In the final scene of *Falconer,* Farragut has made good his escape in the coroner's sack that was supposed to contain a deceased prisonmate. A stranger at the bus stop near the prison pays his fare and provides a raincoat. He even gives him a telephone number in case Farragut needs help. Aboard the bus, the two men shake hands, and the redeemed prisoner feels a strange exhilaration.

> Farragut walked to the front of the bus and got off at the next stop. Stepping from the bus onto the street, he saw that he had lost his fear of falling and all other fears of that nature. He held his head high, his back straight, and walked along nicely. Rejoice, he thought, rejoice. (P. 211)

Indeed! Could anything be more suitable, with a sign of Jonah pointing the way?

Chapter V

A Word
to the Brood
of Vipers

Matthew 23:29–39

Does Jesus' gospel of unconditional admission into the kingdom eliminate the wrath of God? If his stern word to the "brood of vipers" is taken seriously, this question must be reconsidered from start to finish: "You serpents, you brood of vipers, how are you going to escape being sentenced to hell?" (Matt. 23:33). Obviously Jesus was convinced that the attitudes and actions of reptilian humans would provoke an inevitable retribution. No viper would be able to escape it.

When we examine the theologies popular in our time, two opposite approaches to this question become visible. Evangelicals like Billy Graham take the wrath very seriously. His book *World Aflame* insists: "The Bible teaches that God is indeed a God of judgment, wrath and anger" (p. 214). Liberals, on the other hand, tend to emphasize the mercy of God to the practical exclusion of wrath. When Schubert Ogden in *The Reality of God* describes the "promise of faith . . . that we are all, each and every creature of us, embraced everlastingly by the boundless love of God" (p. 220), it is difficult to see how any fragment of wrath can remain. Which of these views is truer to the message of Jesus? And if, as it seems, each is attempting to be faithful to at least one aspect of Jesus' message, is there a basic contradiction within that message itself? Did Jesus' warning to the brood of vipers violate everything he stood for in the Nazareth synagogue?

I

A careful examination of Jesus' word to the brood of vipers takes us into a realm far deeper than traditional arguments between liberals and conservatives. It turns out to be a freshly prophetic message, as challenging to current dogmas as it was to those of the first century.

The first thing we need to consider is that the "brood of vipers" whom Jesus addressed were neither atheists nor religious opportunists. Jesus identifies them plainly as the religious leaders of his day: "Woe to you, scribes and Pharisees, hypocrites!" With such a slashing attack, it is easy for us to fall into stereotypical judgments. But it is clear from everything we know about first-century Judaism that the scribes and Pharisees were not insincere and venal leaders. They would compare favorably with the best of our leaders today. They ranged from liberals to conservatives; they obeyed the laws they taught to others; they were sincerely committed to their religious factions and to their nation. If these leaders were measured by the best of our current standards, not one of us could fairly conclude that they were "hypocrites" in the usual sense of the word.

What then did Jesus have in view? He depicts the problem with a brilliant, one-line citation of the motivation of the scribes and Pharisees in building tombs and monuments for the prophets. "If we had lived in the days of our fathers, we would not have taken part with them in shedding the blood of the prophets" (Matt. 23:30). Now, at first glance there seems to be nothing at all wrong with such piety. How many times have we said similar things? If we had walked where Jesus walked, we surely would not have shouted, "Crucify him!" in the Jerusalem streets. . . . Nor would we have deserted him and denied him as Peter and the rest of the disciples did at the time of the crisis! Or to bring the alibi closer to home: *We* surely would not have taken part in the bloody persecution of Protestants or Catholics during the

religious wars. . . . *We* would not have condoned the burning
of Salem's witches, or the slaughter of the Indian women and
children at Sand Creek, or of the families at My Lai. . . . If
we had been at one of those places, we perhaps would not
have been able to stop the atrocities, but we surely would not
have taken part! What is so wrong with thinking such
thoughts? What could be more natural?

It is therefore puzzling that Jesus goes on to charge those
who boast that they would not have taken part in the atrocities of their forefathers: "Thus you witness against yourselves, that you are the sons of those who murdered the
prophets. Fill up, then, the measure of your fathers. You
serpents, you brood of vipers, how are you to escape being
sentenced to hell?" (Matt. 23:31–33.) What is going on here?
What is there about boasting that they would not repeat the
bloody mistakes of their forebears that makes them similar?
Jesus seems to be turning logic and psychology upside down.
We declare we would *not* participate in such bloody persecu-
tions, would *not* condone our fathers' deeds, and Jesus claims
that those very statements show we are just like "those who
murdered the prophets." We are "their children" in spirit as
well as deed, who *would* in fact be likely to repeat their
actions when the occasion presented itself. The entire passage
that follows in Matthew 23 fills in the details.

The key here is in claiming to be on God's side. The
forefathers of the first-century Jews *had* hounded Jeremiah
to the dungeon and finally to exile and death. They *had*
placed the aged Isaiah inside a hollow log and sawn it in two
lengthwise. Such deeds in retrospect *were* against God's will,
and when the claim is made that they would not have par-
ticipated, it means they would have been on the right side of
those decisions—on God's side. And it is *this* claim, Jesus
charges, that lies at the heart of murdering the prophets.

Why? Because if we are convinced we are on God's side,
in tune with his truth, and thus immeasurably superior to all
those who oppose God's will, is it not logical to be upset at
upstart prophets who declare we are wrong? If we are on
God's side, our competitors must surely be heretics, atheists,

subversives, and perhaps even the agents of demonic forces. There is only one fate suitable for such scum—death.

So there you have it. In a breathtaking reversal the argument runs full circle and at the conclusion leaves you facing in the opposite direction. Those who boast loudest that they are on God's side turn out to be the most deeply opposed to God! We who feel most strongly that we would not repeat the mistakes of our forebears are the very ones most likely to do so. We who would never kill the prophets are apt to do just that.

It is a shocking revelation, a turnabout in perspective that drives each one of us to acknowledge the deeper, more zealous logic of the human heart. It is so simple, yet so far reaching. The logic is nowhere more succinctly portrayed in American literature than in Flannery O'Connor's story entitled "Revelation." Mrs. Turpin, an oversized farmer's wife who takes pride in her charities, hard work, and high moral standards, is in a doctor's waiting room with an assortment of unpleasant and bigoted people. Their laughter at a racial joke and the lyrics of a gospel song on the radio "turned her thoughts sober. To help anybody out that needed it was her philosophy of life. She never spared herself when she found somebody in need, whether they were white or black, trash or decent. And of all she had to be thankful for, she was most thankful that this was so." (Pp. 202f.)

However there was a white-trash woman with soiled clothing in the doctor's office, who had said blacks should be sent back to Africa. When she tried to dominate the conversation, Mrs. Turpin found herself thinking a strangely vicious thought. "If I was going to send anybody back to Africa, . . . it would be your kind, woman." An ugly and hostile college girl in the waiting room seems to sense the discrepant connection between Ruby Turpin's humane creed and her disgust for trashy sinners. The girl's eyes rivet the uncomfortable farm woman with a baleful stare. The girl's well-dressed mother says there is nothing worse than a complaining, ungrateful person, like a certain girl she knows. Mrs. Turpin replies with her most pious tone, "If it's one thing I am,

. . . it's grateful. When I think who all I could have been besides myself and what all I got, a little of everything, and a good disposition besides, I just feel like shouting, 'Thank you, Jesus, for making everything the way it is!' " (Pp. 206f.)

At that instant, the girl's book flies across the waiting room to strike Mrs. Turpin above her left eye, and the girl lunges across the coffee table to choke her. Before being subdued and taken to a psychiatric ward, the coed whispers a line that proves to be a turning point in Mrs. Turpin's life: "Go back to hell where you came from, you old wart hog" (p. 207). It is a charge in the tradition of the "brood of vipers," implying that this paragon of farm-style saintliness is somehow promoting deviltry and filth. Her superior sense of never stooping to the impiety and indecency of others is leading her to thoughts and attitudes fully consistent with devils and pigs.

The image of a viper's brood would have carried a clear connotation of Eden's serpent in the mind of Jesus' audience. It implied that the piety of the scribes and Pharisees was leading an entire generation to repeat the fall of Adam. It stimulated the illusion of moral superiority that leads, ever since the story of the original garden, to death. Whenever religious leaders instill in their followers a pride in never repeating the sins of others, they become vipers, compounding the corruption of an already fallen world. There is more than an echo of such viperdom in the debates between theologians in which each claims to be on God's side. Such claims are frequently made in connection with arguments concerning the end times. For instance, in a book by MacArthur and others entitled *The Rapture,* it is claimed that "Christians who are looking for a return of the Lord are students of prophecy" like the authors, who are "willing to accept the Bible as it is written." On the other hand, "Believers who are looking for the coming of our Lord are never found in the camps of the Modernists, Higher Critics, Unitarians, or Evolutionists." (P. 32.) In other words, only fundamentalists like the authors of the book will be on God's side when the last trumpet sounds.

Ken Sumrall in a more recent book states the idea of divine favoritism more directly: "Are we aware of the fact that a special crown is to be bestowed upon the saints who have 'loved and longed for his appearance'?" (P. 29.) The appeal of the rapture doctrine is closely associated with this kind of certainty. Everyone who has decided to be on God's side, and has subscribed to a certain set of beliefs and actions, will be spared the conflagration at the last minute. They believe that as God's favorites they will be snatched out of the pain of history. In other words, it will pay to be on God's side. That this is the basic appeal of advent preaching is frankly admitted by some of these writers. Herbert Lockyer states that true millennialists like himself have "the conviction that there is no message that arouses the consciences of the lost like that of the return of the saviour in flaming fire to take vengeance on all those who reject the Gospel." In view of his certainty of being on God's side, he finds it inconceivable that anyone would oppose such a message: "What one cannot understand is how professing Christians, with their Bible before them, can yet despise, discredit, and reject the Advent testimony!" (P. 29.)

If what Jesus said about claiming to be on God's side is correct, such preaching is instruction in viperdom. It encourages the very kind of self-righteousness that marked some scribes and Pharisees. It encourages a mentality that will condone the killing of the future prophets. But that is not all.

II

In Matthew 23, Jesus connects the viperous conviction of being on God's side with historical catastrophe. He refers to the terrible vengeance that was to "come upon this generation," describing Israel's "house" or Temple as "forsaken and desolate." When one places these remarks in the context of his weeping over Jerusalem and his warnings about entering into the disastrous war against Rome, their meaning is plain. Whenever people gain the conviction that they are on

God's side, and that consequently they will never fall into the
mistakes of their fathers, they bring catastrophe upon themselves. Jesus had a realistic and historical concept of wrath.
As he saw it, wrath would take the form of historical retribution. And part of the horror of his words stems from the fact
that Israel did declare war upon Rome before that generation
was over. Convinced that they were on God's side, and that
he always favors his elect no matter what the military odds,
they committed a kind of national suicide. A modern person
viewing the smoking ruins of the leveled city of Jerusalem
and the uncounted bodies lying about when the Romans were
through would have thought he was witnessing the scene of
a nuclear holocaust.

Wrath is a historical reality directly related to human
pride, and nowhere in the annals of prophetic literature do
we have a more penetrating treatment of the issue than here.
Jesus' word to the vipers stands as a rebuke to the shallow-
ness of much modern thought. Liberals and secularists have
tended to bypass the idea of historical wrath, assuming that
history can be manipulated by goodwill or technology. Conservatives and fundamentalists have tended to emphasize
wrath in the next life rather than in history. They would note
with satisfaction Jesus' wording in Matt. 23:33, "How are
you to escape being sentenced to hell [Gehenna]?", overlook-
ing the very real historical hell that Jesus had in mind
throughout these Jerusalem warnings. Billy Graham insists
in *World Aflame* that "the Bible has a great deal to say about
hell. No one spoke more about hell than Jesus did and the
hell He came to save men from was not only a hell on earth."
(P. 69.) This traditional perspective allows one to swerve
away from Jesus' powerful doctrine of historical wrath and
talk about the more comfortable business of God rewarding
those on his side with heavenly bliss and punishing his enemies with eternal fire. But as Matt. 23:37ff. makes plain,
Jesus' real concern was the threatened city of Jerusalem and
its "children" who were bound for the dump heap of
Gehenna, the smoldering image of the wrath that strikes
down the illusions of nations or groups that fancy themselves

safely on the side of the angels.

There has been abundant confirmation of Jesus' unexpected prophecy in the twentieth century. That a belief in being on God's side is conducive to a kind of self-imposed historical wrath was perfectly plain in the blasted trenches of World War I that marked the beginning of our modern era. The French, certain that God was with them and that they would not repeat the defensive mistakes of 1870, threw themselves with religious élan against the machine gun emplacements on the frontier and lost almost 300,000 men in the first weeks of the war. The Germans marched into battle singing hymns and wearing belts marked *"Gott mit uns"* and lost 1.8 million men before the horror was ended. The Russians and the Austrians were blessed by their priests for the holy war, and were slaughtered by the millions. The British, so confident that history was on their side and that God would always smile on the Empire, were permanently demoralized by the loss of almost a million soldiers.

In World War II, it happened all over again. The Japanese, certain that the divine power of the rising sun was guiding their victorious troops, fought the Chinese, the colonial powers, and finally the Americans, only to lose everything. An estimated 1.8 million Japanese lost their lives in the war, and their cities looked like the burned-out image of Gehenna when it was over. The Germans, certain they could avoid the mistakes of their fathers while engaging in a two-front war, and confident of divine aid against a godless enemy, invaded Russia and were ultimately thrown back with bitter losses. Uncounted civilians lost their lives in the conquered territories, victims of invading rape and pillage. And then, having failed to detect the lesson of national pride leading to disaster, the French began their atrocious campaigns in Vietnam and Algeria soon after the close of World War II, ultimately losing both. The United States, confident that it was God's favored nation, experienced its first defeat at the hands of a small jungle nation, dishonoring itself in the process.

The lesson of history is that no one is immune to the law

of historical wrath. No nation presuming to be on God's side can long avoid the sentence to Gehenna. But this is not to say that historical punishment is ever precisely proportionate to guilt. There is in fact a kind of avalanche principle at work in history, as Jesus attempted to explain to his listeners. The reference to Gehenna is followed by a remarkable discussion of collective guilt. In Matt. 23:34 Jesus predicts that the conviction of being on God's side would inevitably produce more atrocities against the prophetic messengers. These lines were undoubtedly taken by the early church to refer to the Jewish harassment of Christian missionaries, and it is possible that this experience influenced the final wording of the verse to some degree. But in the following verse there is a chilling threat that "upon you may come all the righteous blood shed on earth, from the blood of innocent Abel to the blood of Zechariah the son of Barachiah, whom you murdered between the sanctuary and the altar" (Matt. 23:35). In other words, the level of pain and destruction threatening Israel would not merely be proportionate to its recent arrogance. The disaster would be boundless, as if all the bloodshed of history were being avenged. Innocent men, women, and children would be slaughtered and there would be no talk about tit for tat. Historical wrath comes crashing down like an avalanche, sweeping away innocent and guilty alike. Like the wall of water cascading from the collapse of the Toccoa Falls dam in the fall of 1977, even the most pious students of God's word would be swept away, their cries muffled by the roar of the night.

The realism of Jesus' word is striking. How can one speak of proportionate wrath in the disasters our century has witnessed? Are the deaths of the innocents in the air raids and the conquered territories of Europe and Asia remotely proportionate to the guilt of individual citizens? To think such a thing is to lose all faith in the justice of God, as some serious thinkers have already done in the face of Auschwitz. Can there be any moral equivalent for the burning to death of thousands of helpless civilians in Hamburg, Dresden, Berlin, Tokyo, Hiroshima, Nagasaki, and Hanoi? No, these are the evidences of avalanching wrath which, once set off by the pride and foolishness of humankind, sweeps indiscriminately through history. As Jesus said by way of warning his fellow countrymen, *"All* this will come upon this generation." That is, all of the untold guilt of past generations was to come upon them to an extent that could never be commensurate with exact justice.

This powerful and realistic insight into the lava-like flow of historical wrath is particularly relevant for our nuclear age. There are some who hope to control the destruction through new weapons like more accurate rockets or neutron bombs. Others conceive the possibility of protecting key populations in underground shelters. Most Americans have grown so accustomed to the threat of nuclear destruction by now that they assume it somehow will never strike us. Robert J. Pranger's "Nuclear War Comes to the Mideast" assumes that an Arab city might be destroyed in an atomic exchange, but that an escalation would not take place. It is reassuring to be told that others will suffer while we will remain exempt, but in the long light of history, it sounds like a grand illusion. And then there are those who remain obsessed with the idea of escaping such a holocaust by means of the Rapture. They would welcome a worldwide conflagration because it would confirm once and for all the invulnerability of true believers. Lockyer's *The Rapture of Saints,* for example, claims with all sincerity that the church will be snatched from the flames just in time. "Our own prayerful study of Holy Writ leads us to believe that the Church will not pass through the period known as the 'Great Tribulation.' In the mercy of God she is to be delivered from its horrors. . . . We are covered by the blood of the Lord Jesus Christ." (P. 62.)

Confidence in the Rapture is greatly at variance with what Jesus was saying in Matthew 24. He foresaw that there would be no escape, no neat separation between the innocent and the guilty. "Alas . . . for those who give suck in those days!" Once started, like the avalanche of A.D. 66–70, the devastation of atomic warfare in our own time would be utterly indiscriminate. No one would be able to stop until the other side's potential for further attacks was completely destroyed. This is why Jesus was so fierce in addressing the scribes and Pharisees. He hoped to avert the deluge! He did not believe it was inevitable, especially if the arrogance that threatened war could be changed in time to a realistic and responsible kind of humility. The will of God visible in the ministry of Christ was that the escalation of violence should never begin. Despite human failures and all the shortcomings of the wicked city, it could yet be spared. It was only the refusal to change that made the destruction inevitable.

At this point we must attempt to clarify the position of Jesus in relation to divine compassion and divine wrath. Clearly it was the compassion of Christ that led him to focus his ministry on averting the wrath. But when a nation refuses to come to its senses and insists on going to the brink, believing that God will somehow direct the disaster to strike only others, the results become unavoidable. But this still does not mean that wrath is a precise embodiment of the divine will. The laws of cause and effect at work in an avalanche do not become vindictive, selecting the guilty and sparing the innocent. God's will in such affairs is life; it is human pride whose fruit is death.

In view of Jesus' stern emphasis on human responsibility, the popular notion that history is determined by God's hatred of his enemies and protection of his friends is a travesty. The current perspective about the Rapture, filled with vindictive dreams of selective punishment, encourages irresponsibility about history and prideful illusions about the security of the saints. J. Dwight Pentecost's *Prophecy for Today: The Middle East Crisis and the Future of the World,* for instance, encourages readers to believe they can avoid the agonies of the last days. "If you are without Jesus Christ when He comes in the clouds to take the redeemed to Himself, as He removed Lot from the scene of judgment, you, like the inhabitants of Sodom, will be left behind for judgment. We invite you to accept Jesus Christ as your personal Saviour that you might have the promise of deliverance from the wrath to come." (P. 59.) This kind of reasoning has the capacity to lead its adherents right into the trap of the scribes and Pharisees. It instills the kind of pride that erodes historical responsibility and prepares the way for the avalanche that may end all avalanches.

III

The proper image for human responsibility in our passage is therefore the hen with her brood. "O Jerusalem, Jerusalem, killing the prophets and stoning those who are sent to you! How often would I have gathered your children together as a hen gathers her brood under her wings, and you would not!" For all those who are committed to a vindictive concept of God, or to a notion that Christ was more concerned about the next world than about this one, these words must come as a shock. Jesus' response to the murdering perversity of Jerusalem was *not* that it deserved to be punished. The yearning of Christ was not to destroy the scribes and Pharisees, but to protect them. They were among the "brood" he had sought to keep alive, along with their wives and children. Far from seeking the end of the world and the punishment of the city, despite all its wickedness and obduracy, he aimed to protect its life.

The feminine image of the hen is one of compassion and defensive realism. Despite the obvious pathos of Jesus' words, it is not a sentimental image. Hens follow a practical instinct in keeping their chicks from harm. They run from danger, shunning conflict at any cost. It is not a foolproof method of protection, but it works well enough to be a fairly good model. It is certainly superior to the proud image of the gamecock. No one who understands this image will waste time spinning tendentious theories about how bad chicks get eaten and good chicks do not. Hens act inclusively, using the humble means at their disposal to protect the life of all their brood. This is precisely what Jesus himself was doing with his message to the leading thinkers of his time. His words about the dangers of believing oneself to be on God's side, of the

indiscriminate quality of wrath, and so forth, were forms of
hen's work, aimed at saving the brood.

Counterpoised against this homely image of the hen is the
image of the Temple that follows in the next sentence. Two
words make the contrast complete—"forsaken" and "desolate." "Behold, your house [i.e., the Temple] is forsaken and
desolate" (Matt. 23:38). The first adjective depicts the loss of
the Temple's role as an agency of intercession and communion between God and man. If God forsakes the Temple,
such communion is no longer possible there. The house of
God becomes an empty shell. The second adjective, "desolate," is a clear reference to its imminent destruction. The
sentence is formulated in the classical prophetic style, as if
the destruction had already taken place. The evasion of
proper responsibility, noted at the conclusion of the preced-
ing sentence with the words, "And you would not!" makes
the doom unavoidable.

To grasp the contrast between the hen and the Temple as
images of responsibility for the future of the city, we need to
examine the role of the Temple in Jewish religion. The chapter by Prof. Safrai on "The Temple" in *The Jewish People in
the First Century* describes it as central in the spiritual life of
the people whom Jesus was addressing. The daily sacrifices,
the elaborate system of liturgical celebration, and the public
instruction in the Torah that took place on the Temple
grounds evoked the passionate loyalty of worshipers. Pilgrimages of faithful Jews occurred at the seasons of the great
festivals, all aimed at taking part in the glorious services. The
ritual life of synagogues led by Pharisees throughout the
civilized world was coordinated with the Temple, while the
ritual within the Temple itself followed regulations worked
out in part by the party of the Pharisees. The passionate care
evident in the Temple activities reveals the belief that God
dwelt there and that his unique favor toward Israel as well
as the eternal redemption of each individual depended upon
the services that assuaged his wrath. The historian Safrai
concludes that "in the eyes of the people it constituted primarily the divine dwelling-place of the God of Israel which

set them apart from other nations" (p. 906). In this regard the Temple stood for the dogma that God was on the side of Israel; it was the image of Jewish superiority which remained intact despite all talk about the services benefiting all mankind. Gentiles were forbidden by pain of death from entering the holy rampart on which the sanctuary stood.

Despite the tragic consequences during the earlier Babylonian era of believing that the Temple and its city of Jerusalem were invulnerable, the belief apparently had reawakened in Jesus' day. So long as the Temple rites were faithfully performed, the living center of religious and political life was thought to be safe. To cite Safrai once again, "It was firmly believed that the Temple was destined to exist eternally, just like heaven and earth" (p. 906). This belief was sustained by the conviction that the entire universe including the heavenly host was involved in the Temple rites. The vessels and the vestments of the high priest were understood to symbolize the cosmos. It therefore appeared inconceivable to the audience Jesus was addressing that anything could fundamentally shake the security of the Temple and those who depended on its services. As the site of the Temple, Jerusalem would remain inviolable. The rabbis came to interpret references like I Chron. 29:11 as if the eternal glory of God rested there. Charif and Raz provide a startling translation of this verse: "... and eternity ... that is Jerusalem" (p. 20). This helps explain the suicidal lack of political realism as well as the appalling religious vacuum that appeared when the Temple was destroyed in A.D. 70. A final summation by Safrai helps place Jesus' prophetic message in perspective: "With the destruction of the temple the image of the universe was rendered defective, the established framework of the nation was undermined and a wall of steel formed a barrier between Israel and its heavenly father" (p. 906).

The alternative Jesus posed was therefore fundamental: either choose himself as a model of henlike responsibility, gathering the helpless brood under protective wings, or choose the Temple as the guarantee for the superiority of the chosen people. Either choose an ethic of compassion or a dogma of divine favoritism. To reject the former was to choose the latter, and this spelled doom. It meant buttressing the psychology of being on God's side with an elaborate theology of divine obligation to the Temple and all it stood for. The result was that the dogma of the eternal Temple made national pride more rigid and disaster more sure.

This may seem rather far removed from our time, for we have no national temple. We make no pilgrimages to a spot where animal sacrifices and burnt offerings are continually dedicated to God. In our day it is dogmas such as the necessity of belonging to some elect community and earning the Rapture that play the role of the Temple, confirming the superiority of the righteous and promising final protection from harm. To belong to such a sect, to recite its beliefs in certain ways, and to hold some theory about the sequence of the Second Coming, is interpreted as placing one in a superior position as God's friend. Membership in such a group becomes a kind of insurance policy that guarantees a safe snatching from the doomed city just before its destruction. Whenever this kind of dogma takes possession of one's mind and heart, the image of the hen and her brood is repudiated.

How much of the henlike compassion of Jesus, for example, do you see in the following?

> The Christian is not to be disturbed by the chaos, violence, strife, bloodshed, and threat of war that fill the pages of our daily newspapers. We know that these things are the consequences of man's sin and greed. If anything else were happening, we would doubt the Bible. Every day we see a thousand evidences of the fulfillment of Biblical prophecy. Every day as I read my newspaper I say: "The Bible is true."

For this preacher, the fate of helpless chicks pales into insignificance compared with the dogma of Biblical predictions about the end of the world. A smug kind of shoulder-shrugging is recommended for true believers because each murder and battle is a sign of divine wrath against evildoers, a confirmation of the great separation between the goats who are doomed and the sheep who possess the correct dogma. The source of these and the following lines is *World Aflame* by Billy Graham (p. 184), the foremost preacher of our day. His grudging support of the henlike efforts of international law are a logical corollary of this perspective. "Can the United Nations save the world from war?" he asks. "The answer is No! It was conceived and created by statesmen who knew little of the significance of the Biblical concept of history and the nature of man. . . . I have supported the United Nations because it offered some hope of at least solving some problems and postponing some major hostilities . . . but the human equation is still there. . . . The superstructure of the United Nations, in its gleaming building on the East River in New York City, has been built on the cracked foundation of human nature. At best, it is only a temporary stopgap." (P. 183.)

A "temporary stopgap"—what better definition could one find for hen's wings? Anyone who hopes for anything more than that from institutions of law and order is deluding himself. There are and will be no perfect and permanent solutions to the problem of human conflict until history comes to its end in God's good time. Meanwhile the best protection for the innocent is a compassion on the part of responsible citizens that leads to steady, enthusiastic support of the imperfect institutions of international order. The most promising institutions of government become ineffective without the commitment of well-informed citizens; witness the demise of perfectly reasonable democratic constitutions throughout Latin America in recent decades; witness the weakening in the peace-keeping capacity of the United Nations since the time of the Korean War, when American public support began its steep decline.

Given the commitment and energy required to keep the institutions of henlike order alive, the lukewarm support of mainline Christians is little better than the angry denunciations of international cooperation that mark the broad spectrum of current watchers for the Second Coming. For example, a Spire Christian Comics version of Hal Lindsey's

There's a New World Coming pictures "the trend to a one-world government" as a demonic sign of the imminent return of Christ (p. 7). Lurid brochures like "The Beast" by Jack T. Chick consistently picture international cooperation and future forms of international government as the work of the Antichrist (p. 21). None of these voices shares the hope of Jesus that hen's wings may yet prevail. None of them agree with his conviction that submitting to international law and order, even when imperfectly embodied in institutions like the Roman Empire, was a better hope than any apocalyptic dogma. Obsessed with the matter of ensuring a privileged status in the impending wrath, they lose the capacity to weep over the imperiled city, and thus they hasten the day of its destruction. The preference for the aura of the Temple over the compassion of the hen could easily bring as grim a result for our atomic age as in the time of the scribes and Pharisees.

IV

Jesus' message to the brood of vipers impels us to take up the providence issue with new seriousness. The belief that God directly controls all of history leads to despair when the innocent are destroyed. On the other hand the belief that history is purposeless erodes hope in the cause of justice and undermines the will to struggle for just ends. Langdon Gilkey's *Reaping the Whirlwind* sifts through the centuries of debate on this issue with great care, resorting to the Biblical concept of the relation between divine grace and wrath. The creative will of God establishes institutions of grace and order that provide the basis for human life, but when pride warps the covenant beyond repair, God enters into a war against his people. Wrath is a historical reality directly related to humankind's capacity to bring destruction upon itself. Sin sets historical forces in motion that can destroy any nation, no matter how powerful. Wrath is the indirect action of God in allowing these forces of destruction to converge. "This cycle of gift, sin and catastrophe is," Gilkey writes, "never an inexorable necessity. . . . There is always the possibility Israel will listen to the prophetic word of warning about this grim cycle, and in listening come to repent, to return, and be spared" (p. 262). Human freedom and responsibility play decisive roles in the processes of historical retribution. Even when destruction is inevitable, God is at work offering hope to sustain creative response to the tragedy. Gilkey concludes that this Biblical concept provides the most adequate framework in the modern world, "in terms of which alone the creativity, the sin, the tragedy, and the renewal of hope characteristic of historical experience can be comprehended" (p. 263).

To bring this Biblical perspective into relation with the popular religious impulses of our time requires that both Fundamentalism and liberalism be transformed. Neither is capable of sustaining a fully responsible attitude toward current history. Neither can counter its tendencies to produce broods of vipers. Liberal theology and secular thought in general continue to encourage a strong sense of superiority in their adherents, a feeling of immense freedom from the shackles of traditional beliefs and mores. Some of these spokesmen continue to take delight in shocking the naïveté of the pious, demonstrating through earthy words and actions that they would not have been part of the repression of their forebears. They would never "have taken part with them in shedding the blood of the prophets." This innate sense of being on the right side of things persists even though its premises have eroded in recent decades. Liberal optimism rested on the widely shared dogmas of progress through technology and democracy, the gradual humanizing of history and politics, and the intrinsic goodness of humankind, once the corrupt institutions that hold people in bondage are destroyed.

As these optimistic dogmas become increasingly implausible in the light of twentieth-century experience, elements of despair become mixed with nostalgia for the old reforming spirit. The most popular film of recent years is *Star Wars*, and one of the most acclaimed musicals in the same period is *Little Orphan Annie,* both emblems of the yearning to recapture the simple zeal of earlier liberal culture. They give expression to the key assumption, no longer acknowledged in embarrassing times, that the heroes, the political system, or the church are to bring in the kingdom of God through battling zeal. These popular entertainments express an idea that disintegrated in the misguided crusades of the 1960's, that a battle of the enlightened "good guys" against the depraved "bad guys" will always end up well. Whether it is embodied in liberal politics, religion, or popular culture, we witness an inability to face the avalanche of history, to take seriously the fact that those who presume to be on the side of truth and justice become disaster prone.

But current Fundamentalism seems no more promising. It is more realistic about the sinful qualities of human nature, to be sure. But it confuses the historical consequences of sin with a childish kind of divine pique, as if God hated his enemies and protected his friends. The concentration on the Last Judgment, conceived simplistically as a separation of good guys from bad, tends to weaken the concept Jesus had of historical retribution that falls ever and again through history on complacent and arrogant Jerusalems. Rather than calling people to work responsibly to overcome injustices and nationalistic pride so as to avert such wrath, Fundamentalism has tended to offer an otherworldly escape, a promise of safety in the next life. In so doing it reduces the transforming gospel of Christ to a guarantee of special privilege, a pay-off for copping out of historical responsibility. Sadly, in view of its deep commitment to the Biblical heritage, Fundamentalism tends to be blind to its own pride, its certitude about being on God's side while all others are damned.

An example of this was pressed into my hands recently in the form of a little illustrated tract by Jack T. Chick entitled "Someone Goofed." A cynical spokesman of liberalism blows cigarette smoke in the face of a beleaguered, Bible-quoting Christian while telling him, "Let's face it! The Bible is filled with contradictions, everybody knows it! Our most modern accredited, theologians admit this—it's only written by men!" The boy this cynic leads astray is killed by a train and ends up in hell. The lad points his finger at his betrayer with the charge, "You were wrong—you goofed!" The man pulls off his mask to reveal the face of Satan. (Pp. 3–18.) The message is clear: spokesmen of liberal theology are satanic despoilers of the innocent, while fundamentalists are on the side of heaven. Material like this has a capacity equal to that of arrogant liberalism to turn its devotees into a brood of vipers.

To bring popular religion in America up to the level of Jesus' message requires combining the best of both Fundamentalism and liberalism. We need to join a sense of impending wrath with a grasp of the compassion of God. Moving past dogmas on either side that restrict our realism about history and encourage a fatal sense of rectitude, we need to be drawn by the power of Christ into forms of genuine responsibility for the imperiled city. Impressed by Jesus' preference for the imperfect justice of international government as embodied in the Roman occupation of his country, we need to recapture the momentum of relying on international agencies in the resolution of conflict. The Christian community, having spawned the vision of the United Nations and its associated agencies of international cooperation, must redirect its energies toward strengthening them. Here is the proper avenue for Christian concern for world peace and human rights, not the competitive arena of big-power diplomacy. Christian churches of whatever persuasion must be led to this constructive task if they are to be true to the message of their Master.

The alternative is in danger of being overlooked in the current lull, when military conflicts seem far from the doorsteps of the "Christian" nations of Europe and America. But the echo of Jesus' warning is audible in the arms buildup of developing nations, the escalation of technological stratagems on the part of nuclear powers, and the unresolved conflicts that girdle the globe: "Truly, I say to you, all this will come upon this generation." The stakes are no longer a single city or country, but the atomic despoliation of the

green and blue planet that spins its way in an orbit far distant
from other forms of advanced life that may exist in this
immense universe. There are no political superheroes to save
us from ourselves—only a sense of responsibility that common citizens and leaders may catch. But there is also a vision
—which may prove more powerful than the threatening avalanche—of a broad and pleasant realm where wayward
broods are faithfully gathered under patient wings.

For Jesus' unexpected vision to gain the power to avert the
avalanche threatening our generation, Christians must acknowledge the constant danger of viperdom. As Flannery
O'Connor shows in the final scene of "Revelation," there is
a new freedom and clarity of vision given to those who are
brought to admit the truth about themselves. Mrs. Turpin is
at the concrete hog house, hosing down the swine in the wake
of the fateful revelation in the doctor's office. She yells her
outrage against heaven for sending such an unwelcome and
unfair message. Then, driven by "a final surge of fury," she
roars, "Who do you think you are?" The color of the sunset
"burned for a moment with a transparent intensity" as the
answer came to her. She saw a streak of light extending
upward from the Georgia earth on which a vast company was
moving toward heaven. There were the white trash, "clean
for the first time in their lives," along with blacks in white
robes and lunatics "leaping like frogs." Bringing up the rear
was a tribe of respectable folk like herself, orderly and on key
as usual, yet strangely transformed. Mrs. Turpin "could see
by their shocked and altered faces that even their virtues were
being burned away." As she turned back toward the house,
the crickets took up their evening chorus, "but what she
heard were the voices of the souls climbing upward into the
starry field and shouting hallelujah." (Pp. 216–218.) And
thus in the mercy of God lies the hope of the world, even for
wart hogs and vipers and their broods.

Chapter VI

When the Wood
of the Cross
Is Green

Luke 23:28–31

There have been innumerable books and sermons on the meaning of the cross. Some present elaborate theories of the atonement to explain how it is that Christians sense that Jesus died for us. With few exceptions these theories are based on the affirmations of early Christian believers rather than on things Jesus himself said about his death. So far as I can tell, the word on the green and dry crosses has never figured very prominently in these theories. Yet the most explicit thing Jesus ever said about the meaning of his death was uttered to the women of Jerusalem as he was led by the legionnaires to the place of the skull: "If they do this when the wood is green, what will happen when it is dry?"

As a kind of foil for understanding the current bearing of this unexpected prophecy, I would like to relate it to Walker Percy's novel *Lancelot*. Its protagonist is a modern crusader who is conscious of standing in the succession of those who sought the grail. Two forms of atonement confront each other in this book, just as they did in the streets of Jerusalem: atonement through violence and atonement through sacrificial love. Lancelot tells his priest, Percival, that when the revolution comes,

> We'll take the grail you didn't find but we'll keep the broadsword and the great warrior Archangel of Mont-Saint-Michel and our Christ will be the stern Christ of the Sistine. And as for your

sweet Jesus . . . and your love feasts and peace kisses: there is
no peace. . . . No, it is not you who are offering me something,
salvation, a choice, whatever. I am offering you a choice. Do you
want to become one of us? You can without giving up a single
thing you believe in except milksoppery. I repeat, it was your
Lord who said he came to bring not peace but a sword. We may
even save your church for you. You are pale as a ghost. What
did you whisper? Love? That I am full of hatred, anger? Don't
talk to me of love until we shovel out the————. (Pp. 178f.)

It reminds one of the zealous vision that Jesus was con-
fronting with his strange word about the green wood of the
cross.

I

The women of Jerusalem were weeping as they saw a good
man, an innocent victim, driven to the place of execution.
"Daughters of Jerusalem," he said, "do not weep for me, but
weep for yourselves and for your children. . . . For if they do
this when the wood is green, what will happen when it is
dry?" At first glance this is a puzzling simile. The difference
between green and dry wood is that the one goes up in smoke
more easily. Dry wood burns quickly and well. But what does
burning have to do with the execution of Jesus or the women
of Jerusalem?

There are some clues in this saying that would have been
obvious to Jesus' original listeners but have to be recon-
structed for our modern ears. Often similes like this were
easily understood at the time of their first utterance because
they picked up what people were thinking or had recently
experienced. But a later generation, with other thoughts and
experiences, misses the overtones and thus the point of the
simile. The first clue relates to the connection between "burning" and a cross.

In the first century, Judeans and Galileans knew that
crucifixion was the Zealot's death par excellence. Each Zeal-

ot uprising against Rome was climaxed by crucifying those involved. Anyone taken alive in a Zealot guerrilla raid or assassination attempt was certain to be hanged on the tree. Recent studies of the Zealot resistance movement indicate that the term "robber" was often applied to the guerrillas, probably because they so frequently attacked the rich collaborators of Roman provincial administrators. Josephus consistently calls rebels "robbers" or "brigands," and it is likely that the two thieves executed with Jesus were really thieves of this type. Barabbas, whom the crowd had preferred to have released instead of Jesus, was certainly a Zealot. Luke identifies him as "a man who had been thrown into prison for an insurrection started in the city, and for murder" (Luke 23:19). So Jesus is heading to Golgotha to occupy the cross originally intended for Barabbas. He was facing a Zealot's death, as confirmed by the charge of political subversion placed on the cross: "This is the king of the Jews."

Now, what does all this have to do with burning? The Zealots had a reputation for burning zeal. In fact the very word "zeal" in Hebrew and Aramaic is closely related to what we would term "being hot under the collar." It comes from a root that means "dyed dark red or black," and it connotes the color of the face when one is enraged. Now, in comparison with Zealot wood, which was dry and ready to ignite, Jesus refers to himself as green. He was not one to fly off in murderous zeal. His whole ministry aimed at turning down the burner of zealous hatred and war. In his parables, and probably also in numerous unrecorded discussions and arguments, Jesus had sought to calm the zeal of his own disciples and the crowds to whom he preached. As I show in *The Captain America Complex: The Dilemma of Zealous Nationalism,* Jesus' ministry stood in the tradition of prophetic realism. Some of his best-known sayings directly counter the zealous fanaticism of his own era (pp. 167–175).

One final clue enables us to capture the idea in this unexpected prophecy. Jesus uses the pronoun "they" in this saying: "If they do this when the wood is green, what will happen when it is dry?" Everybody knew who "they" were:

the hated Roman legionnaires, who at that very moment were driving three men to a grim place of execution. The simile deals with what the Romans are doing and will continue to do, with invincible power: stamp out rebellions and crucify the survivors.

Now, to put it back together: "If they [the Romans] do this when the wood is green [i.e., crucify someone who is as unwilling to burn with zealous hatred as I am], what will happen when it is dry?" That is to say: What will the Romans do to your sons and husbands who are plotting right now to engage in a zealous insurrection? They are dry and ready to flash out in zealous flames at any moment. G. B. Caird, a recent commentator on the Gospel of Luke, states the point in a similar fashion: "Israel's intransigence has already kindled the flames of Roman impatience, and if the fire is now hot enough to destroy one whom Roman justice has pronounced innocent, what must the guilty expect?" (Pp. 249f.) Although he associates the fire with Roman rather than with Zealot wrath, the point comes through clearly enough.

The saying about the green wood of the cross thus continues the warnings in the opening words of this unexpected prophecy to the people of Jerusalem (Luke 23:28–31): "Daughters of Jerusalem, do not weep for me, but weep for yourselves and for your children. For behold, the days are coming when they will say, 'Blessed are the barren, and the wombs that never bore, and the breasts that never gave suck!' Then they will begin to say to the mountains, 'Fall on us'; and to the hills, 'Cover us.' " When the Jewish-Roman war breaks out (as it did less than forty years after Jesus' crucifixion), the destruction will be so complete and unavoidable that parents unable to protect their children will wish they had never brought them into the world. Innocent victims will be ravaged and destroyed in the battle and those who survive will face a hopeless life of slave labor until they drop in their tracks. "If they do this when the wood is green, what will happen when it is dry?"

II

What has all this to do with the meaning of the cross? It points toward an arena hardly ever touched in sermons about the atonement. It is far removed from the realm of silvered and fluted crosses that remind us of eternal life in the world to come. It is quite different from the concern for private salvation that surfaces in most of our hymns about the cross. There is no hint in this word concerning the payment of a price for human sin, balancing the scales of divine justice, or the magical power of blood. The arena of Jesus' concern on the way to Golgotha was social and political. He was less concerned about his own fate than about his nation's future. Jesus wanted the tearful witnesses on the Via Dolorosa to draw some conclusions for themselves and for their families. He used this last contact with the Jerusalem crowds to warn them again not to drift toward the impending rebellion against the Roman occupation.

The message about the green wood of the cross sought first to shatter the zealous illusions that so easily lead a country and a world into destruction. The Zealots knew they were outnumbered by the Roman legions. They recognized the inferiority of their weapons and armor. But they counted on the intervention of the heavenly armies to even out the score. At the decisive moment, when the outcome of the battle would be most in doubt, Yahweh the Lord Sabaoth, the commander of the angelic host, would intervene. Like the United States Cavalry or Buffalo Bill's scouts in earlier phases of American imagination, they would charge over the hill into action just as the savage enemies were about to prevail against the innocent. Or like the P51's in the old John Wayne war movies, the winged warriors would fly down from the heavens to rescue the last of the brave Zealots who stood for freedom. The action adventure stories in current entertainments, with superheroic redeemer figures who arrive just in time to save the community, feed the kind of illusion that Jesus had in view.

This illusion is embedded in *Lancelot,* one of the most celebrated novels of 1977. One zealot will be enough, Lancelot Lamar insists, to perform the decisive act of violence that will usher in the new age.

> There is going to be a new order of things and I shall be part of it. Don't confuse it with anything you've heard of before. . . . Don't confuse it with the Nazis. They were stupid. . . . Don't confuse it with the Klan. . . . Don't confuse it with Southern white trash Wallace politics. It's got nothing to do with politics.
>
> It is none of these things. What is it then?
>
> It is simply this: a conviction and a freedom. The conviction: I will not tolerate this age. The freedom: the freedom to act on my conviction. . . . What if one, sober, reasonable, and honorable man should act, and act with perfect sobriety, reason, and honor? Then you have the beginning of a new age. We shall start a new order of things.
>
> We? Who are we? We will not even be a secret society as you know such things. Its members will know each other without signs or passwords. No speeches, rallies, political parties. There will be no need of such things. One man will act. Another man will act . . . and act alone if necessary—there's the essential ingredient—because as of this moment not one in 200 million Americans is ready to act from perfect sobriety and freedom. If one man is free to act alone, you don't need a society. (Pp. 156f.)

The plot of Walker Percy's novel seems to bear out this illusion. Discovering his wife has been unfaithful, and that a degenerate group of film makers he had welcomed into his mansion is corrupting even his daughter, Lancelot uncaps the gas well in the basement on the night of a hurricane and blows them all up after slitting the throat of his wife's lover with a bowie knife. True to the formula of redemption through violence, in which the hero typically escapes, and returns to paradise in the end, Lancelot survives the blast. He is observed for a while in a mental institution and then released, planning to resettle in the wilderness area of Virginia. Fate, as it were, has smiled on the perfect crime, the act of zealous violence against the wickedness of this age, in which all ends well.

It will not be so, Jesus told the daughters of Jerusalem. Fate does not intervene. The heavenly blasters do not fire on schedule, as the demise of the Messiah proved. If the legionnaires could execute God's elect without any divine intervention to stop them, what chance was there for a Zealot uprising? If Jesus proved unable to "come down from the cross," what is the likelihood of a Lancelot Lamar being blown out unscathed in the explosion that destroyed the wicked? How effective is the violence of one man acting "from perfect sobriety and freedom"? "If they do this when the wood is green, what will happen when it is dry?"

Jesus died to shatter the illusions of his generation about the possibility of superhuman agencies saving the people from the forces of history. He died expressing the mercy of the Abba that sustains us in the face of the worst that history can report. But it is sobering to realize that the illusion of escape lives on. It is being popularized with all the sophisticated means of modern film and cartoon techniques. Despite the awesome threats of this atomic age—perhaps in part because of them—Americans today, both inside and outside the churches, cling to images of superheroism. The incongruity is immense. For the past thirty years, the specter of a devastated planet has loomed over us all, with the echoes of burned women and children crying out to the mountains, "Fall on us," and to the hills, "Cover us."

One image has haunted me ever since I read John Hersey's *Hiroshima.* It is the stunned and mutilated streams of civilians stumbling out of the city after the flash more brilliant than a thousand suns. But we console ourselves with the nightly illusions of superheroes and heroines saving their communities from such disasters in the nick of time. The catastrophe films of the past few years nurture the illusion that wise redeemers will contrive to save the innocent by leading them out of a capsized *Poseidon* or delivering them from the uncanny *Jaws.* Similarly, evangelists proclaim a dream of escape in the message about the Rapture of the saints just before the Tribulation in which the wicked will be annihilated. Neither they nor their congregations appear to be aware of the utter disparity between such hopes and the realism of Jesus.

III

Jesus attacked such illusions because they erode the sense of responsibility to do what can be done to avoid historical disasters. Jesus' word to the women of Jerusalem was to take responsibility for themselves and for their families, to influence those around them in the direction of peace. This is the second major point in this unexpected oracle of Jesus.

Calling upon the women of Jerusalem to take political responsibility was in fact one of the most unusual things Jesus ever did. It was not an era in which common people were thought to have significant responsibility in the affairs of state. Only a few Jews in places of authority were actually in a position to exert much influence on the Roman administrators. None of these were women. In the Jewish world, women were expected to refrain from public roles of leadership and responsibility. Yet Jesus addressed them as if they were perfectly capable of assuming responsibility for the future of their country. He urged them to do what they could. And he used the strongest emotional and moral appeal possible in that era of large, tightly knit families: "Weep for yourselves *and for your children.*"

The force of this appeal was in allowing parents to visualize for themselves what it would be like if they let things drift to the point of no return. The vivid picture of parental helplessness was aimed to shock people out of their lethargy, breaking through the stereotypes of role, class, and sex, thus allowing vigorous and imaginative new forms of leadership and responsibility to come to the fore. Even in our current era, which seems so hostile to family life, and in which so many of our most sophisticated young people are opting for a life-style that rules out the nurture of the young, such an appeal retains its force.

The most poignant episode I ever heard about parental helplessness was recounted by a pastor who had invited my wife and me over on a Sunday afternoon, when our studies in Germany were just beginning. We noticed a family picture on the mantle, in which he appeared, standing with a different woman than his current wife. In the picture six or seven towheaded youngsters stood proudly beside their parents. He observed our interest in silence and, after some hesitation, told us what had happened. During one of the bombing raids in World War II he had been on fire watch, guarding the old church in Heilbronn on the Neckar River, when a bomb struck the building and threw him to the pavement. When he stood up again, it was clear that the church was burning too rapidly to be saved. He hurried next door to the manse, where his wife and children had taken refuge in the deep cellar, only to find that the house was also on fire. Through the thick oak doors he heard the cries for help, but when he tried to move the timber that had fallen over the outside entrance, he found that both of his hands dangled helplessly. They had both been broken at the wrist when he fell. The frantic pastor dashed to the street for help, only to find that the firebombs had ignited the asphalt pavement. The city was a solid mass of flames. He returned to his home and stood by helplessly, listening to the shrieks of his wife and children as the flames reached them. The worst thing of all was that there was nothing he could do to save them.

It is important for our generation, just as it was for the daughters of Jerusalem, to visualize the helplessness of such a moment, and to derive from it a realistic sense of responsibility about what can be done now. To weep for ourselves and for our children can shake us into acting before the avalanche begins to rumble. A notable example was Mairead Corrigan's tearful BBC interview in the wake of the smashup of an escaping terrorist car at a schoolyard in Belfast. Richard Deutsch relates how three of her sister's children were killed in this senseless accident. Mairead's voice broke as she told the television interviewer, "It's not violence that people want." Betty Williams, another Catholic woman from Belfast, watched the interview and started a petition campaign. Two days later she found herself on television reading a petition that thousands of women had signed. She said, "I am only the spokesman for many women. . . . These three children must not have died in vain. . . . After such a tragedy, we must and will have peace." (Pp. 4–6.) The two women broke precedents of role definition and religious stereotypes in drawing both Protestant and Catholic women together in a series of peace marches that brought them the Nobel Prize in 1976. Their weeping for themselves and for their children unleashed creative energies no one would have suspected were present, leading to actions that shocked their communities and aroused the conscience of the world. In the face of intimidation, the complexities of a foreign occupation, and the gruesome history of religious warfare in their country, these women and their supporters are continuing to prevail. Though it may take generations to succeed, their effort appears to be driven by what the historical Jesus knew to be a reservoir of moral resolution—the recognition that parents should act before it is really too late.

Perhaps the greatest barrier that such tears must melt is resignation to a seemingly inevitable future. People come to the conclusion that disaster is unavoidable, that hatred weighs too heavily on the scale to be affected by the puny power of love. Consequently there is nothing anyone can do. People feel the weight of public opinion, they remember the failure of their earlier hopes, and they conclude that perhaps violence alone can clear the past and usher in a better future. Such resignation clearly plays a role in the New Apocalypticism, reinforced by the belief that a worldwide Tribulation is predestined by divine will. Although Jesus devoted his final words on the streets of Jerusalem to countering such ideas, they surface over and over again, sometimes in the least likely places.

Walker Percy's novel *Lancelot* is full of such resignation to an apocalyptic future. At one point the indignant hero cries: "I'll prophesy: This country is going to turn into a desert and it won't be a bad thing. Thirst and hunger are better than jungle rot. We will begin in the Wilderness where Lee lost. Deserts are clean places. Corpses turn quickly into simple pure chemicals." (P. 158.) Earlier in the novel, Lancelot Lamar reveals his view of history, one that many people appear to share these days: "Next follows catastrophe of some sort. I can feel it in my bones. Perhaps it has already happened. Has it?" he asks his confessor friend who is able to keep up with news outside of the detention center. "Catastrophe then—yes, I am sure of it—whether it has happened or not; whether by war, bomb, fire, or just decline and fall. Most people will die or exist as the living dead. Everything will go back to the desert." (P. 36.) At the end of the story, having committed the apocalyptic crime fully in keeping with this sense of inevitable disaster, Lancelot asks his confessor the crucial question before he is released.

> I can see in your eyes it doesn't make any difference anymore, as far as what is going to happen next is concerned, that what is going to happen is going to happen whether you or I believe or not and whether your belief is true or not. Right?"
> [The priest replies,] "Yes." (P. 256)

These sentiments are little more than a high culture version of the New Apocalypticism. Both not only reflect certainty of a catastrophic future, but they revel in it. About the only difference is in Percy's honest appraisal of the bloody cost of such zealous redemption, and the necessity of human agencies to bring it about. But the protagonist Lancelot Lamar shares both of the fatal premises that Jesus sought to counter in his own disaster-prone society: a laming sense of inevitability about a catastrophic future and an illusion about the possibility of the elect escaping from that future by means of superhuman intervention.

IV

Having pursued the logic of the green and dry crosses and their relation to current responsibilities, we are now in a position to consider what all this has to do with the atonement. How does the death of the Savior provide atonement for human sin? How does it save humankind? This is a mystifying arena for current faith and theology. Even the word "atonement" has a baffling and perhaps for some an offensive connotation. One thinks of expressions like "saved by the blood" and wonders if anyone can explain their meaning.

The term basically signifies "at-one-ment," overcoming the barriers that keep humans apart from God and from each other. To overcome alienation is to atone. In Jesus' time, human alienation took its most dangerous form in the effort to manipulate God through zealous warfare or legal campaigns to bring in the kingdom. When Jesus suffered the Zealots' fate without deserving it, when he died in place of Barabbas, such alienation was both exposed and overcome. Jesus' word to the women of Jerusalem was aimed at showing how his death on the cross could set them "at one" with God and with history itself. They could realize that he was dying for their sakes, as a result of the courageous effort to turn them back from the brink of national suicide, and thus they might be awakened to an authentic relationship with God and their fellow human beings.

Although there is a profound depth and mystery in the atonement of Christ, I do not believe there is anything magical about it. It does not balance out some distant scale of divine justice, nor does it pay the price of sin to some cruel divine paymaster. The cross is not an entrapment game with the devil, as one of the primitive theories suggests. Christ died for us, and for our sins, in order to turn us and the human race around. As long as our zealous illusions remain intact, neither we nor our children are safe. To be atoned for is to be set "at one" with the Abba's will for his entire planet.

It is to take up the cause of peace and justice wherever we walk in life, to pursue the kingdom of divine righteousness in our vocations and in our homes. It is to give up our illusions of private escape, to repent of our sins and selfishness, and to begin daily living a new life, following the commandments of God who is the parent of all.

I am not suggesting that the atonement's meaning is exhausted by these social and political implications. The rebellion of the human race has individual connotations as well, so that the implications of the cross reach to every area of life. No theology of which I am aware encompasses it entirely or does it full justice. Perhaps only in the riches of Bach's *St. Matthew Passion* or similar works of art does the human mind give adequate expression to this event that stands at the heart of the divine revelation. But I would still insist that the plain words about the green wood of the cross point to an arena of public responsibility that must be *included* in any doctrine of the atonement.

What concerns me most is not that a fully adequate statement of the doctrine is lacking. Some of the most brilliant minds in the history of Christianity have wrestled with this issue, resting content in the end to affirm that there are depths of divine righteousness that can never be captured by their theories. There are times to quit theologizing and begin celebrating. My concern is that an alien concept of atonement has slipped into American religion and now stands not only at the center of the New Apocalypticism but at the center of popular entertainments as well. I refer to atonement through violence, the very doctrine that Jesus sought to counter on the streets of Jerusalem.

I trace the evolution of this doctrine in *The Captain America Complex,* from its origins in Biblical stories like Phinehas' murder of the Israelite and his Midianite wife to its expression in the modern superhero tales (pp. 82–96). Phinehas believed that the plague threatening Israel was caused by intermarriage with foreigners. Taking the law into his own hands, he broke into the marriage tent to kill the offending couple with one thrust of his spear. His "zeal" was affirmed

by the tradition as an expression of divine zeal. Through his
act of vigilante violence he "made atonement for the people
of Israel" (Num. 25:13). This tradition of atonement through
murder stood at the center of the motivation of the Zealots
in Jesus' time, as studies by Martin Hengel make plain. It
assumes a central role in the early Puritans' definition of their
crusading obligations, and is embodied in the Manifest Destiny themes in American history. It was popularized in the
great wars to make the world safe for democracy, and in the
actions of cowboys and cops in the superhero stories, who
shoot down bad guys to save helpless communities.

It is perhaps surprising to anyone who has not studied the
origins of the macho-redemption tales in popular American
culture, but such tales can be traced to the same strand of
Biblical thought that produced the New Apocalypticism
(*The Captain America Complex,* pp. 27–56). The central
texts for the formative Puritan preaching during the Colonial
era that shaped the American redeemer nation ideology were
Daniel, Deuteronomy, and Revelation. The same materials
animate the New Apocalypticism. And the products are
strikingly similar, even though the one is explicitly religious
and the other is classified by most people as "mere entertainment." Both favor a stereotyping of the opposition, a conspiracy theory of evil, a conviction that the good side always
wins, and a certainty that violence is finally redemptive.
While the proponents of the New Apocalypticism yearn for
a nuclear conflagration of the planet that will cleanse it of evil
once and for all, the fans of *Star Wars* cheer the explosion
that destroys the evil Death Star that was threatening the last
outpost of a brave rebel force. Although these materials may
appear at first glance to be worlds apart, their origins are in
the very tradition that the historical Jesus feared would lead
his generation into the abyss.

The danger of the New Apocalypticism is therefore not
simply that it popularizes an ideology that has repeatedly led
to disaster in the past, but that it converges with the most
popular public entertainments of our time. Each lends power
to the other, the explicitly religious providing the ultimate

justification for violence itself, and the entertainments providing appealing heroic images of its enactment. What we have most to fear from this convergence is that the rejection of Jesus' warning to the women of Jerusalem will lead to its violent alternative. We reject an atonement through suffering love because we are so deeply committed to the seemingly more satisfying drama of atonement through violence. Perhaps this is due in part to the sense in which atonement through love is more threatening, more terrifying, more challenging to the armor we erect around ourselves, than all the earthquakes and plagues of apocalyptic wrath.

One of Flannery O'Connor's most shocking stories revolves around the problem of the atonement, and its ultimately threatening quality. "A Good Man Is Hard to Find" tells of a grandmother on a vacation trip with her son and his family. On the way to Florida, she cajoles her unwilling son into turning off the road in search of a lovely plantation house she had seen as a girl. On the deserted back road the car tips over. Three men come upon the scene of the accident, and she recognizes the leader.

> "You're The Misfit!" she said. "I recognized you at once."
> "Yes'm," the man said, smiling slightly as if he were pleased in spite of himself to be known, "but it would have been better for all of you, lady, if you hadn't of reckernized me." (P. 22)

He is the psychopathic killer whose reported escape from a nearby prison had been the talk of the travelers.

As the companions of The Misfit take the other members of the family for walks into the woods, followed by pistol reports, the kindly grandmother alternately pleads for her life and tells her captor that he should pray to Jesus for help. He replies, "I don't want no hep. . . . I'm doing all right by myself." (P. 26.) He describes his conviction that atonement, especially in the penal system, is never commensurate with the wrongs one has committed. "I call myself The Misfit," he says, "because I can't make what all I done wrong fit what all I gone through in punishment." The problem with Jesus

is that he "thrown everything off balance. . . . Jesus was the
only One that ever raised the dead, and He shouldn't have
done it. He thrown everything off balance. If He did what He
said, then it's nothing for you to do but throw away everything and follow Him, and if He didn't, then it's nothing for
you to do but enjoy the few minutes you got left the best way
you can—by killing somebody or burning down his house or
doing some other meanness to him. No pleasure but meanness." (Pp. 27f.)

It was clear to him that if Jesus' atonement were real, the
life of killing would have to end. He bent close to the grandmother and said with intense emotion that he wished he had
been there to see if Jesus were real: "If I had of been there
I would of known and I wouldn't be like I am now." At this
instant she was moved by a flash of parental affection for The
Misfit, whose agony was so apparent. But her gesture threatens his defense system more than all the blank walls of the
prison he had escaped.

> She saw the man's face twisted close to her own as if he were
> going to cry and she murmured, "Why you're one of my babies.
> You're one of my own children!" She reached out and touched
> him on the shoulder. The Misfit sprang back as if a snake had
> bitten him and shot her three times through the chest. Then he
> put his gun down on the ground and took off his glasses and
> began to clean them. . . . Without his glasses, The Misfit's eyes
> were red-rimmed and pale and defenseless-looking." (Pp. 28f.)

At the end of this terrible story, we find ourselves sus-
pended like The Misfit between a violent atonement that both
attracts and repels us, and a loving atonement that threatens
to penetrate our armor and reveal that we do need "hep"
after all. To refuse to admit our vulnerability, denying any
impulse to weep for ourselves and for our children, leaves us
on the track that leads from Phinehas to The Misfit, from the
crusades of the knights in armor to the modern Lancelots
who blow up their friends to bring in "the new order of
things." O'Connor was as clear-eyed as the historical Jesus

in seeing where such decisions can lead. For despite all the allure of heroic fantasy, and all the certainty of the New Apocalypticism, the road of atonement through violence proves hard on children and grandmothers. The better alternative was offered by the man whose warnings still haunt the streets of the holy city. The question is whether we can break free to act on the basis of his concern for the children of Jerusalem . . . and of Heilbronn . . . and of Hanoi . . . and of Sioux City. "For if they do this when the wood is green, what will happen when it is dry?"

Chapter VII

The Feast of Enemies or the Rapture of Escape

Luke 22:14–27

Religious rapture is a conspicuous feature of popular religion in the final quarter of the twentieth century. One thinks of the excitement of the charismatics who gathered at Kansas City in the summer of 1977, forty thousand Christians of various denominations celebrating their unity in Christ. Many thousands of others have experienced similar moments of great exaltation at Holy Spirit Conferences or Lay Witness Missions across the country. But for some Christians the ultimate Rapture is yet to come. Based on an archaic translation of I Thess. 4:17, the doctrine of "the Rapture" teaches that true believers will be lifted bodily into the heavens just before the Tribulation that will destroy most of the planet. As Hal Lindsey told a television interviewer who wondered how he could avoid utter despair as a member of *The Terminal Generation,* "I expect to be evacuated from this planet in a mysterious way before the worst part of this breaks loose" (p. 173).

The depiction of the Rapture has long exercised an appeal to Christians in the English-speaking world. A book written by James H. Brookes in 1874 sounds remarkably like the ones now crowding the shelves of Christian Book Stores. It conveys the thrilling expectation of an event that was expected to happen in Brookes' lifetime:

O, what rapture shall thrill the hearts of the redeemed, what ecstasy of bliss shall ravish the sorrowing, tempted, troubled disciples of Jesus, when responding to His shout that will sound to the world only as a strange clap of thunder, they shall in a twinkling of an eye be changed into the likeness of His glorious body, and together with the risen saints, hand in hand with some whose graves have cast a shadow all along their pathway of life, they shall ascend to be with Him forever, and to be done with sin and suffering forever! (P. 533)

The escape from earthly trials is particularly appealing when troubles mount. A college student told me recently that whenever he feels swamped with work and discouraged with studies, he wishes for the Rapture. But when things are going well, he is happy that the world continues along as it does. Since these are troubled times, just as Brookes's era was, the appeal of the Rapture doctrine is very strong.

To suggest that the historical Jesus was against the Rapture as currently defined does not imply that God in his mysterious way is unable to make good come out of such preaching. As Hal Lindsey says in *The Terminal Generation,* "Concentrating on what God has promised in the Rapture produces amazing transformations in motivating people to live for Christ" (p. 178). Who can doubt the impact of images like those in Lindsey's Spire Christian Comics version of "There's a New World Coming"? One section of this issue entitled "The Great Snatch" consists of shapely blond girls in short skirts along with handsome young men whose arms are thrown back in the ecstasy of being lifted up to the heavens while their unenlightened friends ask, "W—What's going On?" The answer is "The Rapture!!!" (Pp. 3–4.)

I would like to relate this to another kind of rapture—the joyous celebration of the messianic banquet in the teachings and ministry of Jesus. In the accounts of the Last Supper we gain a clear impression that it was a "feast of enemies," where the tensions and differences between the disciples was once more overcome by the love of him who said, "This is my body. . . ." To grasp the distinctive form of rapture evoked

by Jesus' meals with his friends, it is necessary first to un-
cover the ecstatic anticipation of first-century religion. This
involves removing layers of pious dust from the tradition of
the Lord's Supper.

I

The image most Christians have of the Last Supper is
indelibly stamped by Leonardo da Vinci's somber and formal
scene of the long table with six disciples on each side of their
master. It has all the spontaneity of a head table on the
chicken-dumpling circuit. The artist manages to allow each
person in the masterpiece a distinctive expression of chagrin,
perplexity, or conspiracy, but there is no hint of rapture. This
image is consistent with the celebration of the Lord's Supper
in most contemporary churches. For the most part it is sol-
emn, guilt-ridden, somewhat dull, and blessedly infrequent.
The joyous atmosphere of early Christianity, which continued the sometimes raucous celebrations of Jesus and his
disciples, is conspicuously lacking. Arthur Cochrane's study,
Eating and Drinking with Jesus, suggests as a remedy incor-
porating the Sacrament into the eating of an actual meal
together. This would be a step in the right direction. But
breaking the loaf and blessing the cup at the end of a parish
potluck dinner would be a mere shift of form if there is not
a recovery of the intense expectation of the kingdom of God
as a banquet.

It is clear that Jesus' contemporaries associated God's
kingdom with a feast. When a pious Pharisee sitting at the
banquet with Jesus uttered his ecstatic beatitude, he used the
terminology typical for the first century: "Blessed is he who
shall eat bread in the kingdom of God!" (Luke 14:15.) In his
Eucharistic Words of Jesus, Joachim Jeremias has provided
a number of parallels to this statement. I Enoch 62:14f. predicts that when the Messiah comes, the elect will share in his
banquet: "And with that Son of Man shall they eat . . . and
the righteous and elect shall have risen from the earth, and

ceased to be of downcast countenance." A rabbinic saying promises the participation in such a meal for those who obey the law: "Those who serve God unto death, will eat of the bread of the world to come in plenty." After surveying the wide range of metaphors used in apocalyptic, Rabbinic, and Christian literature for the messianic meal, Jeremias concludes: "In whatever way the metaphor is presented, the meaning is always that divine gifts are imparted in eating and drinking." (Pp. 233f.)

The centrality of the banquet image for Jesus and its connection with the Isaiah prophecies are explicitly affirmed in his statement to the Roman centurion who had faith that his servant would be healed. "Not even in Israel have I found such faith. I tell you, many will come from east and west and sit at table with Abraham, Isaac, and Jacob in the kingdom of heaven." (Matt. 8:10f.) The enemy peoples from the ends of the earth, who had formerly been barred from eating with Jews because of legal restrictions and the long tradition of enmity, would come to the messianic table. The terms of this powerful vision of a feast of former enemies stem from Isa. 49:12 and 25:6–8, with the latter assuming a particularly central role in Jesus' proclamation and disclosure of the kingdom.

From the references to the Gentiles in the Isaiah prophecies it is clear that the messianic banquet was to be a feast of enemies. As Jesus appropriated the prophecies for his own ministry, the return of the Jews from their homeless wandering would be combined with a conversion of the very Gentiles who had harassed them for generations. "All peoples" would join the feast at the Lord's table. The language of the Isaiah 25 prophecy is instructive:

On this mountain the LORD of hosts will make for all peoples a feast of fat things, a feast of wine on the lees, of fat things full of marrow, of wine on the lees well refined. And he will destroy on this mountain the covering that is cast over all peoples, the veil that is spread over all nations. He will swallow up death for ever, and the Lord GOD will wipe away tears from all faces, and the reproach of his people he will take away from all the earth; for the LORD has spoken.

The "veil" in this passage is the barrier to communication and insight, the nationalistic wall that separates each nation and people from its neighbors and from God. With its disappearance, genuine dialogue between former enemies would commence around the Messiah's table. And there is no doubt that the feast would be celebrative. The most expensive oils and wines would flow in abundance. As Bernhard Duhm's classic commentary suggests, this vision "differs very decisively . . . from the terrible particularism of later centuries. . . . It is an abundant and expensive meal of fat, which as the best portion of the animal otherwise belongs to God, and of wine on the lees" left for an unusually long period to gain strength and sweetness (p. 156). It would make quite a party.

I encountered these expressions for strong drink at the time of my doctoral exams in Tübingen. As the custom was, I went a week or so ahead of time to discuss with the professors what I had been studying. I told the Old Testament professor I had been working recently on Daniel and he suggested that I also prepare the related material in Isaiah 25 to 28. Naturally I agreed, not wanting to reveal any weaknesses in my knowledge of how to translate Hebrew into German. I went back to my room and looked over the Isaiah material. It was appalling to find so many words I had never seen before. I began desperately compiling new vocabulary lists. With the expressions in Isaiah 25, I even had to find an English dictionary to grasp the idea. My teetotaling upbringing in a Methodist parsonage had prepared me well for life, but not for understanding "wine on the lees well refined"! I passed the oral exams—barely—and now have a clearer sense of the celebrative connotation of the strange vocabulary. In the poverty-stricken milieu of late Judaism, these images meant overcoming want and necessity, regaining prosperity and the productivity of the land, and therewith the means to provide a feast fit for kings but enjoyed by all. Judging from the way Jesus followed out this vision in his festivities with publicans and sinners, it clearly implied a messianic celebration that could break down barriers between in-groups and their enemies.

The widespread assumption of ancient and modern times, of course, is that this kind of celebration can only occur after the apocalyptic battle is over. The book of Revelation places the beatific scene after the Battle of Armageddon, as do all the writings of the New Apocalypticism. First-century Judaism shared this assumption completely. One of the Rabbinic sayings cited by Hans Conzelmann in Kittel's *Theological Dictionary of the New Testament* is the following: "Joy in this world is not perfect; but in the future our joy will be perfect." That is, when the Messiah has vanquished his enemies, unreserved celebration will be possible. One of the Rabbinic sayings insists, "It is joy before God when those who anger Him vanish from the world." The messianic context of these utterances becomes clear in a midrash on the Song of Solomon: "But when they [the prophets] say to you: Lo, thy king comes to thee, righteous and full of salvation, they will then say: This is a perfect joy" (pp. 364f.). One reason religious leaders in Jesus' era were so scandalized at his joyous celebrations was the conviction that one should not rejoice "before the time," that is, before the climactic battle with evil had been won. A similar idea is embodied in the most popular film of our time. *Star Wars* concludes with a great celebration in a cathedral-like hall, in which the heroes are invited forward to be honored by the princess. The countless rows of warriors, the triumphant remnant of the "brave rebel force," cheer because they have succeeded in winning this cinematic equivalent of Armageddon. Luke Skywalker has succeeded in blowing up the Death Star with his atomic torpedo, so joy is now allowed. It is a theme that unites the popular entertainments and popular religion of this and probably every age.

The outrageous thing about Jesus' celebrations was that they were staged *before* evil was destroyed. In opposition to the popular religion of his time and ours, Jesus brought the

banquet of Isaiah into the homes of Simon the Pharisee and
Zacchaeus the tax collector and the various other locales of
his itinerant ministry. The shock waves of this messianic
strategy are visible in charges like "Behold, a glutton and a
drunkard, a friend of tax collectors and sinners!" (Matt. 11:
19) and "Why do . . . your disciples . . . not fast? (Mark 2:18).
The purpose of fasting, for the Pharisees and for John the
Baptist, was to atone for the sins of Israel that had brought
defeat and degradation. If the wrath of God could be impelled to lift, because of the repentance of his people, then the
messianic age might begin; God would vanquish their enemies and fasting could give way to celebration. But to celebrate now, before such a turn of fortune occurred, appeared
presumptuous and subversive. Jesus' reply to the dour and
deadly refusal to celebrate in the present was characteris-
tically witty and unanswerable: "Can the wedding guests fast
while the bridegroom is with them?" (Mark 2:19.) If the
Messiah is here, the time for enjoying the banquet with him
is now. To fast under these conditions is absurd. In the words
of the wedding song that Jesus' hearers would have known,
"the time of singing has come, and the voice of the turtledove
is heard in our land" (Song of Solomon 2:12).

Jesus' strategy was simple but profound: celebrate God's
presence now in the messianic banquet, prior to the destruction of evil, and evil will be transformed by the celebration
itself. The incredible effect of this strategy is visible in stories
like the conversion of Zacchaeus, a tax collector hated by his
fellow countrymen (Luke 19:1–9). Rather than denouncing
Zacchaeus or supporting the Zealot campaign of ritual assassination for him and his family, Jesus invited himself into the
rich man's house for the messianic banquet. The crowd
"murmured" at this outrageous acceptance of a sinner who
was betraying his country by collaborating with the Romans.
They would have preferred the sequence of material like the
Qumran "War of the Sons of Light and the Sons of Dark-
ness": first destroy evil in an effective military campaign and
then start thinking about the victory celebration. But Jesus'
strategy effected a voluntary transformation on the part of

Zacchaeus that all the physical force in the world could not have achieved. Feeling unconditionally accepted into the banquet, and thus assured of a place among the people of God, his defenses and hostilities collapsed. He began a life of caring for his fellow countrymen whom he had formerly exploited. In his *New Testament Theology,* Jeremias describes this approach as a "proclamation of forgiveness in action." "To understand what Jesus was doing in eating with 'sinners,' it is important to realize that in the east, even today, to invite a man to a meal was an honor. . . . Thus Jesus' meals with the publicans and sinners, too, are not only events on a social level, not only an expression of his unusual humanity and social generosity and his sympathy with those who were despised, but had an even deeper significance. . . . The inclusion of sinners in the community of salvation, achieved in table-fellowship, is the most meaningful expression of the message of the redeeming love of God." (Pp. 114–116.) The inclusion of outcasts like Zacchaeus living in Galilee and Judea would be the first step in fulfilling the prophecy about the feast of enemies at the end of time.

There is a kind of contemporary Zacchaeus tale in Saul Bellow's *Henderson the Rain King.* It is a hilarious novel about a blundering giant of a man who fought his way through the first half of his life seeking the acceptance the tax collector had experienced in a single afternoon. "I thought myself a bum and had my reasons, the main reason being that I behaved like a bum," Henderson says on the opening page of the novel. He had once read the hopeful word he needed, but then forgot which book it was in, searching fruitlessly for years to find it again: "The forgiveness of sins is perpetual and righteousness first is not required" (p. 3). He ultimately finds such unmerited forgiveness expressed in the life of a wise African chief and is enabled to find himself in a form of the feast of enemies. As he returns home at the end of the novel, altered and committed to serving others, the reason is clear: "Whatever gains I ever made were always due to love and nothing else" (p. 339). It was a love he had to

experience rather than simply read on a page in his father's book. And it is this love that was conveyed in the
remarkable celebrations during the ministry of the historical Jesus.

II

The strategy of redemption through celebration is a kind
of touchstone linking many of the most important themes
and actions in Jesus' ministry. It is visible in the parables
about banquets and celebrations and in numerous conversa-
tions reported in the Gospels. It plays a crucial role in the
episode of the cleansing of the Temple, which was the immediate provocation leading to the cross. Acting on the popular
hatred of foreigners, the money changers had encroached
upon the Gentile court of the Temple, thus occupying the
only spot where non-Jews could participate in the Temple
worship. Jesus drove them out while citing from Isaiah a
reference to the Temple as a "house of prayer for all the
nations" (Mark 11:17; cf. Isa. 56:7), thus expressing the need
to retain that powerful symbol of the equality of all enemy
peoples before God. It was the very spot mentioned in Isaiah
25, "on this mountain," where the messianic feast of enemies
would occur. In a very real sense, Jesus died in the service
of this redemptive vision.

In the Lord's Prayer there is a daily reminder of the
centrality of the feast of enemies. The original connotation of
the "daily bread" petition was that the end-time banquet
should become a present reality. As Jeremias shows in *The
Proclamation of Jesus,* the literal translation would be "Tomorrow's bread, give us today!" It is the bread of the kingdom, of the messianic feast, that is in view here. Disciples are
to pray that the meal at this morning's breakfast table, or the
snack at the hamburger shop, be made into a celebration of
the kingdom. "For Jesus, there was no opposition between
earthly bread and the bread of life. . . . For the disciples of
Jesus, every meal, and not only the last one, had deep es-

chatological significance. Every meal with Jesus was a salvation meal, an anticipation of the final feast." The bread petition, Jeremias explains, "does not tear apart the everyday world and the heavenly world, but asks that in the midst of everyday secularity the powers and gifts of the coming world may be effective." (Pp. 199f.) When this petition is granted, the kingdom manifests itself anew in a feast of enemies that transforms the participants into friends.

It appears that Jesus' strategy of fulfilling the Isaiah prophecy of the messianic feast was directly related to the peculiar method of gathering disciples. As Martin Hengel has shown in his untranslated study, *Nachfolge und Charisma,* the approach of Jesus to discipleship differed radically from either the master-pupil relationship favored by the rabbis or the commander-warrior concept of the revolutionaries. Rather than simply attracting followers, from whom brilliant pupils could be selected to undergo lengthy study as the Pharisee masters did, Jesus *chose* his disciples in an arbitrary manner. Rather than stirring up masses of followers by martial rhetoric and prophetic demonstrations as the apocalyptic prophets and messianic pretenders did, he *called* them one by one, creating a circle of twelve to call all Israel into response to the kingdom. The fact that other disciples accompanied Jesus, including several women in the inner circle, has led some scholars to believe that the calling of the twelve was a fiction of the early church. But the uniqueness of the selection method and the rapid separation of the Twelve after the crucifixion and resurrection forbid this conclusion. Hengel argues rightly that the Twelve were chosen on the model of Old Testament prophets to serve the kingdom (p. 81), but he does not relate this to the strange disparateness of those selected. I believe that an examination of the party affiliations of the Twelve reveals an intention to guarantee that the celebration of the messianic banquet would be a genuine feast of enemies.

Despite the conflicts and variations in the New Testament lists of the twelve disciples, one thing is clear. They were not "birds of a feather" flocking together. A more varied, if not to say motley, group could hardly have been imagined in the context of the first century. There was Matthew, sometimes identified as Levi, a tax collector and collaborator with the Roman provincial administration. There were four fishermen, Peter, Andrew, James, and John, typical examples of the lower-class "people of the land" who were viewed as sinners by the religious establishment and troublemakers by the bureaucrats. At least two persons in the circle had been associated with the Zealot resistance movement: Judas Iscariot, whose strange second name was probably a transcription of *sicarius,* meaning "assassin," and Simon the Zealot, sometimes called Simon the Cananaean, from the technical term in Aramaic for a Zealot revolutionary. There was Philip, who came from a family with Hellenistic aspirations, given the Greek surname. There were Thomas and Thaddaeus, both of whom are sometimes identified as Judas the son of James. And finally there was Bartholomew, possibly identical with Nathanael, the upstanding middle-class figure referred to in John 1:45–51. The precise identification of these twelve men is less significant than their diversity, which would have been stunning in the first-century context. The groups from which they came hated each other with a sometimes maniacal fury. We know that the Zealots and the bureaucrats were engaged in a brutal struggle of assassination, purge, and ambush, It is reasonable to expect that sensible middle-of-the-roaders despised the extremists on both sides.

One thing is certain: representatives of these groups would never have voluntarily joined one another in common meals or causes. The walls of exclusion were abnormally high in first-century Palestine. They had to be called, impelled into the kingdom by the charismatic power of an enormously attractive messianic figure. Their very selection by Jesus bears the distinctive stamp of his idea about how the Isaiah 25 prophecy would be fulfilled. He wanted the messianic feast to be truly inclusive, linking mortal enemies around a single table as an emblem of the reconciliation that marks the kingdom of God. These mutually hateful representatives of the ideological parties that would later destroy one another in the Jewish-Roman war were transformed by eating together day after day, their celebration of the kingdom breaking down the barriers that had stood between them. The most sensitive point in first-century social relations, the kosher food laws that separated saint from sinner, was attacked not so much by discussion as by practice. Celebration was allowed to break down the inhibition that piety had imposed, so that unconditional acceptance into the kingdom was experienced with all its shocking power. Not only were they invited to eat together, sharing a common purse and table, but the motley dozen of the transformed were led with other disciples and adherents from house to house in the amazing pilgrimage. They ate one day with sinners and outcasts, the next with Pharisees, and the day after with wealthy representatives of the political establishment. They joined in wedding festivities and in the meals of commoners. Wherever they ate, it was clear that mere satisfaction of hunger was less crucial than the celebrative joy. The symbolic circle of the Twelve represented Israel in all its divisions and types, joining in the feast of enemies with the first of the east and the west that would soon encircle the globe.

In the Last Supper there was a remarkable embodiment of the idea of fellowship, around a table, that reconciles competitors and enemies. There is no doubt that the meal reported in Luke 22 was a Passover celebration, but too little attention has been given to the remarkable transformation that occurred. Jeremias argues strenuously in *The Eucharistic Words of Jesus* that the Last Supper was a genuine Passover meal. Many of the sayings attributed to Jesus during this meal are adapted from the Passover liturgy and bear the stamp of the distinctive Aramaic style of speaking that was characteristic of him. But instead of symbolizing the lamb's blood spread on the lintel of the houses to warn the destroyer to pass over the elect while killing the firstborn of Egypt, the cup was given to the disciples as a symbol of him who would shortly die for the sake of the kingdom. The unleavened bread, instead of symbolizing the hurried escape of the elect from the oppression of Egypt, represented the broken body of the Messiah given for saint and sinner alike. These changes of an originally nationalistic rite, involving the violent destruction of enemies and the achievement of freedom for true believers, move it in the direction indicated by all of the earlier celebrations Jesus had inspired. One of the early studies of the Aramaic background of the Last Supper appears to be more sensitive to this crucial issue than recent studies have been. Gustaf Dalman's *Jesus-Jeshua,* first published in English in 1929, points to alterations that reveal the distinctive view of Jesus. Jesus was dissatisfied with the traditional Passover because it lacked "the perfectly experienced fatherly love of God. In His [Jesus'] expectation, therefore, everything racially-narrow and legally-formal, and everything of this earth earthly, is set aside before the great reality of the sovereignty of God, which will then determine resolutely that which is inward and that which is outward." (P. 184.) The language Dalman uses is somewhat romantic, but the point is clear: Jesus transformed the rite of nationalistic escape into a feast of enemies.

III

The theme of reconciling enemies is prominent in Luke's account of the Last Supper. The warning to Judas in Luke 22:21f. and the admonition to the squabbling disciples in vs. 24–27 reveal Jesus' ongoing effort to bring about the transformation of the messianic feast. These words express the reconciling power that underlies all of the elaborate theories about the Sacrament; they counter forms of enmity that are a constant threat to genuine Christian rapture.

The conflict among the disciples concerned the question of status. "A dispute also arose among them, which of them was to be regarded as the greatest" (Luke 22:24). This kind of competition, as characteristic of primitive tribespeople as of sophisticated moderns who claw their way desperately to the top of the economic, social, or ecclesiastical ladder, poses a fundamental threat to the equality of kingdom membership. If admission to the messianic banquet is free to all, if the inverted kingdom is genuinely open to those without status or accomplishment, then competition at the table is a violation of its nature. Hence Jesus points out the pagan quality of status-seeking, along with its capacity to camouflage itself by the rhetoric of service and leadership. "The kings of the Gentiles exercise lordship over them; and those in authority over them are called benefactors. But not so with you." (Luke 22:25f.) In a circle of pious patriots, these words must have come as a shock. The very exploitation and hypocritical sloganizing they had come to hate in their Roman overlords are here exposed in their own petty squabbles.

The main character in Saul Bellow's novel *Henderson the Rain King* admits that a demand for status lies at the heart of his violent antagonism against the world. His early and unsuccessful competition with his brother for the affection of his father had left a voice that haunted him for years. Henderson says: "There was a disturbance in my heart, a voice that spoke there and said, *I want, I want, I want!* It happened every afternoon, and when I tried to suppress it it got even stronger. It only said one thing, *I want, I want!*" (P. 24.) He took outrageous steps to quiet this voice, including learning to play his father's violin. He drove his family crazy with the clumsy sawing away with his massive hands, but the voice did not go away. Henderson admitted, "My main purpose was to reach my father by playing on his violin." Even after his father's and brother's deaths, Henderson kept on practicing. "Down in the basement of the house, I worked very hard as I do at everything. I had felt I was pursuing my father's spirit, whispering, 'Oh, Father, Pa. Do you recognize the sounds? This is me, Gene, on your violin, trying to reach you.'" So he played on, "keeping time with the voice within." (P. 30.) But as with the disciples in the final supper with their Lord, the voice kept on and on, creating enmity and senseless competition that ruined everything.

The immediate provocation in the case of Luke's account of the strife at the Last Supper was the warning about an imminent betrayal. The consternation among the disciples caused by Jesus' announcement that "the hand of him who betrays me is with me on the table" (Luke 22:21) has often been depicted by expositors and artists. But the motivation of the warning is worth reflecting on: Unless Jesus wanted to provoke self-righteous strife among the Twelve, which seems unlikely, his intent must have been to warn Judas not to pursue the plan that he had devised. The fatal conflict with the authorities was unavoidable, he implied, so nothing will be gained by assisting them. "For the Son of man goes as it has been determined; but woe to that man by whom he is betrayed!" (Luke 22:22) Given the Zealot background of Judas, it is not plausible that he would have cooperated with the authorities out of sympathy for their aims. It is more likely that he remained true to his zealous ideology, believing that when the final crisis came, Jesus would be forced to resort to the traditional messianic violence to bring in the kingdom. The subsequent insistence by Jesus that the disciples take swords to the nighttime vigil on the Mount of Olives, and his dramatic repudiation of their use in an act of Zealot resistance against the authorities, suggest such an interpretation. If Judas believed that he was acting in the best interest of the messianic kingdom, that the Master would be forced to call down legions of angels to start the expected revolution, the warning makes sense. His zealous idealism was misguided, the warning implied; if he persisted, it would be a betrayal that would bring woe upon Judas himself.

The subsequent fate of Judas confirms the suggestion of misguided zeal. According to Matt. 27:3–5, he became convinced of his error after the capture of Jesus and tried to return the reward money he had received. He threw the thirty pieces of silver on the floor of the Temple chambers and "went and hanged himself." These are not the acts of a person motivated by greed or cynicism. They reveal a discovery of fundamental betrayal and enmity against God, central issues that everyone must face, particularly when committed to apocalyptic schemes to bring about the Battle of Armageddon. But in the context of the Last Supper, it is clear that the aim of Jesus was the same as throughout his ministry: to reconcile human beings to the ways of God and to each other. In short, it was to make the feast of enemies a reality.

The humane contribution of Bellow's novel *Henderson the Rain King* is to transform the theme of misguided idealism into something we can laugh at and even recognize in ourselves. While we would resist acknowledging the shadow of Judas across our face at times, it is easy to identify with Henderson's admission that he had muffed all the crusades in his life: "I seem to have the Midas touch in reverse," he tells his African friend Romilayu (p. 113). He had just tried to play the role of rain king, using a homemade gunpowder bomb to kill the frogs polluting the cattle cistern of a drought-plagued tribe. He succeeded only in blowing out the retaining wall at the front end of the reservoir and allowing the entire water supply to disappear into the sand. One of the most hilarious scenes in modern literature is that of Henderson desperately trying to shore up the rapidly emptying reservoir, the frogs pouring into his trousers and shoes, and the cattle bellowing against their tethers for the water that would soon be gone forever (p. 109). Following this disaster, he moves on to another tribe, participates in their rain dance, and then accompanies the chief, Dahfu, who miraculously appears to have mastered the entire tradition of Western and Eastern wisdom.

The question of bringing enmity to a halt is discussed by Dahfu and Henderson before they undertake a fatal lion hunt. The wise chief argues that "there is a law of human nature in which force is concerned. Man is a creature who cannot stand still under blows. . . . In the beginning of time there was a hand raised which struck. So the people are flinching yet. All wish to rid themselves and free themselves and cast the blow upon the others. And this I conceive of as the earthly dominion." (P. 213.) Henderson surprises himself by replying that some people return good for evil, and the chief agrees: "A brave man will try to make the evil stop with him. He shall keep the blow. No man shall get it from him, and that is a sublime ambition. So, a fellow throws himself in the sea of blows saying he do not believe it is infinite. In this way many courageous people have died." (P. 214.)

It is only after Dahfu is killed on the lion hunt that Henderson is able to carry through with this idea of responsible reconciliation in his own life. The old chief courageously takes his place in the lion trap, manipulating the precarious contraption to drop a net over the cornered prey. He understands the risk of failure, but is determined to be responsible to his own destiny and to his people, despite all their incomprehension and hostility. "Well, Henderson, what are the generations for?" Dahfu asks. "Only to repeat fear and desire without a change? This cannot be what the thing is for, over and over and over. Any good man will try to break the cycle. There is no issue from that cycle for a man who do not take things into his hands." (P. 297.) Dahfu falls within reach of the lion while trying to release the net, and Henderson is shocked and grieved into taking responsibility for his own life. "I slept through my youth," he confides to the stewardess on the plane going home. "I'm eager to know how it will be now that the sleep is burst." (Pp. 334f.) He plans to enter medical school at the age of fifty-five, serving others rather than himself, trying his best to "make the evil stop with him." It is perhaps not as far removed as one might think from the strange transformation that finally came upon those who realized, after the bloody work was done, what was meant by the words spoken in an Upper Room, "This is my body."

IV

The issue motivating my concern about "the Rapture" as currently taught is that it rejects this message of reconciliation. It seeks to pass the blow on. It not only promises superior status to those who believe but it betrays the task of reconciling enemies, the very task that Jesus died to achieve. It translates the hurt and blows each person inevitably receives in this life into a program of cosmic vengeance. As the bumper stickers proclaim, "In case of Rapture, this car will be unoccupied." In other words: You other drivers on the interstate who have scorned the New Apocalypticism will soon be dodging giant hailstones and nuclear mushrooms. . . . When you face the Tribulation, you will wish you hadn't been so critical. . . . We are taking our blows now, but you'll soon get yours. And so the succession of blows moves on, presumably into eternity, unaltered by the reconciling feast.

When one examines the original textual basis for the doctrine of the Rapture, a similar turning aside from the central message of the faith is visible. The idea arises from I Thess. 4:16ff., where Paul is assuring his people that when the Parousia occurs, they will not be separated from loved ones. "And the dead in Christ will rise first; then we who are alive, who are left, shall be caught up together with them in the clouds to meet the Lord in the air; and so we shall always be with the Lord. Therefore comfort one another with these words" (I Thess. 4:16–18). These statements were made necessary, as Ernest Best shows in his recent commentary, by the fear on the part of early Christians that they would indeed be separated when the end came. Some congregational members had died, unexpectedly, and those who were left had the odd conviction that they would never meet again. Paul's intent is to provide "comfort," not the basis of an elaborate new doctrine.

The ultimate irony of the doctrine of "the Rapture" is that it alters what was originally intended as a metaphor of togetherness into a theology of separation and escape. That believers would be rejoined with their loved ones when the end of time came was the clear implication of I Thessalonians. It is transmuted now into a belief in separation between saints and sinners, with the true church being released from the Tribulation that will punish those who disagree with certain theological points.

The appeal of this theology of escape is shown clearly by Jack T. Chick's illustrated booklet, "The Beast." A pious wife tells her cynical husband that "the Rapture . . . could happen tonight and I'd be gone! I wish you'd surrender your life to Christ—before it's too late!" He dismisses this with one wave of his cigarette-holding hand, scarcely looking up from his *Playboy* magazine: "C'mon, now, Do you *actually* believe that yarn about Jesus raising the dead believers and the *real* Christians off the earth? Haw. Haw. *That'll* be the day!" (P. 13.) A few days later the same man is shown with sweat pouring down his brow after calling for his wife who has mysteriously disappeared from her kitchen. "Oh my God— Where's my wife?? All of the REAL Christians *are* gone!— the Rapture came, just like she said it would!" (P. 18.)

While there may be a few persons who are pressured into repentance after reading such pamphlets, it seems clear that the basic appeal is to those who already believe. It is highly attractive to picture yourself as having the final word in disputes, imagining that your opponents will one day realize how right you were. It is a yearning not unrelated to the competition for status among the disciples. The doctrine of the Rapture not only appeals to those who have a sense of status deprivation; it justifies and confirms such feelings with elaborate teachings about the superior position of the true believers in the divine plan. As Guy Duty insists in *Escape from the Coming Tribulation: How to Be Prepared for the Last Great Crisis of History,* "Those who obey the Bridegroom's command to be ready when He comes will share the privilege of reigning with Him forever in His 'kingdom wherein dwelleth righteousness' " (p. 86). To use the expression employed when children play, "I got first dibs."

I do not deny the presence of such feelings or the need to cope with them, but I am convinced that the gospel of unconditional acceptance into the kingdom is a much healthier and more profoundly transforming remedy. The message of the unexpected prophecies of Jesus is that the higher rapture is available here and now, each time we join in the feast of enemies. Its mood is typified by the words spoken by the disciples after the meal at Emmaus with the strange person who joined the conversation about the Messiah's coming. He made himself known in the breaking of the bread, and afterward they said to each other, "Did not our hearts burn within us while he talked to us on the road, while he opened to us the scriptures?" (Luke 24:32.) Is it really possible for those who have taken part in the feast of enemies to continue yearning for the rapture of escape? Is it suitable for those who want a truly opened Scripture to reject the banquet? Is it for us to deny the larger promise that those who partake of the single loaf become "one body"? (I Cor. 10:17.) To accept this higher rapture is to live out the life of reconciliation, to enjoy the unity that is beyond all competitiveness and status-seeking. It is not only the higher rapture, but the only rapture worth seeking. As for our reunion with loved ones at the end of time, that will be taken care of in the Lord's own way.

There is an image of rapture at the end of *Henderson the Rain King*. Henderson has befriended a Persian orphan on the plane back to New York. When they land in Newfoundland, the two go out to stretch their legs. At the beginning of the novel, Henderson had been unable to sympathize with his daughter's instinctive love for a foundling child. The child was of a different race and he found himself unable to touch it. Now, redeemed through the blood of the great chief and purged of the voice crying "I want, I want," he is able to comfort the boy whose language no one knows and whose name is simply pinned to his coat with a safety pin.

> So we were let out, this kid and I, and I carried him down from the ship and over the frozen ground of almost eternal winter, drawing breaths so deep they shook me, pure happiness, while the cold smote me from all sides through the stiff Italian corduroy with its broad wales, and the hairs of my beard turned spiky as the moisture of my breath froze instantly. . . . I told the kid, "Inhale. Your face is too white from your orphan's troubles. . . ." I held him close to my chest. He didn't seem to be afraid that I would fall with him. While to me he was like medicine applied, and the air, too; it also was a remedy. . . . Laps and laps I galloped around the shining and riveted body of the plane, behind the fuel trucks. Dark faces were looking from within. The great, beautiful propellers were still, all four of them. I guess I felt it was my turn now to move, and so went running —leaping, leaping, pounding, and tingling over the pure white lining of the gray Arctic silence. (Pp. 340f.)

If the Rapture does not include fifty-five-year-old millionaires and lost orphans from the Orient, it is not worth sharing. But it does. We who are close to the kingdom may act like broods of vipers at times and refuse the upside-down celebration. We may wish we had a great deal more to go on than signs of Jonah, that our means of coping exceeded mere hen's work. There will be times when we prefer that the battle with Satan were still in the future, and that some of our competitors would be discomfited in the process. But the feast that started in the peasant villages of Galilee goes on, and he who makes himself known in the breaking of the bread strides on before us, uniting us all.

The challenge of his unexpected prophecies is to accept the transforming rapture ever and again. For the oracles are addressed to each of us: not just to fundamentalists, or liberals, or evangelicals, or Catholics, or Orthodox, or whatever, but to all who wish to gather at his table. Despite our differences, the word of reconciliation can yet be heard. And those who receive it will be led to a prayer that the day may swiftly come when all creatures will ascend to the mountain of the Lord and join the feast "of fat things full of marrow, of wine on the lees well refined." In the meanwhile, we can practice what we pray: Give us this day the bread of the morrow . . . the loaf that makes us one!

References

Barr, James. *Fundamentalism.* Westminster Press, 1978.

Becker, Ernest. *Angel in Armor.* George Braziller, 1969.

Belk, Fred Richard. *The Great Trek of the Russian Mennonites to Central Asia 1880–1884.* Herald Press, 1976.

Bellow, Saul. *Henderson the Rain King.* Viking Press, 1959; Penguin Books, 1978.

Best, Ernest. *A Commentary on the First and Second Epistles to the Thessalonians.* Harper and Row, Publishers, 1972.

Boice, James Montgomery. *The Last and Future World.* Zondervan Publishing House, 1974.

Briggs, Kenneth A. "Charismatic Christians Seek to Infuse the Faith with Their Joyous Spirit." *The New York Times,* July 22, 1977.

Brookes, James Hall. *Maranatha: or, The Lord Cometh.* St. Louis: Bredell, 1874.

Caird, G. B. *Saint Luke.* 1963. Westminster Pelican Commentaries. Westminster Press, 1977.

Charif, Ruth, and Raz, Simcha. *Jerusalem the Eternal Bond.* Tel Aviv: Don Publishing House, 1977.

Cheever, John. *Falconer.* Alfred A. Knopf, 1977.

Chick, Jack T. "The Beast." Chino, Calif.: Chick Publications, 1966.

———. "Somebody Goofed." Chino, Calif.: Chick Publications, 1972.

Cochrane, Arthur C. *Eating and Drinking with Jesus: An Ethical and Biblical Inquiry.* Westminster Press, 1974.

Cohn, Norman. *The Pursuit of the Millennium.* Essential Books, 1957.

Conzelmann, Hans. *"Chairō."* In Rudolf Kittel (ed.), *Theological Dictionary of the New Testament,* Vol. IX, pp. 359–372.

Cranfield, C. E. B. *The Gospel According to Saint Mark.* Cambridge: University Press, 1959.

Creed, J. M. *The Gospel According to St. Luke.* London: Macmillan & Co., 1960.

Dalman, Gustaf. *Jesus-Jeshua: Studies in the Gospels.* Tr. by P. P. Levertoff. 1922. Eng. tr. 1929. KTAV Publishing House, 1971.

DeHaan, Richard W. *Israel and the Nations in Prophecy.* Zondervan Publishing House, 1968.

Deutsch, Richard. *Mairead Corrigan, Betty Williams.* Tr. from the French by Jack Bernard. Barrons Educational Series, Inc., 1977.

Duhm, Bernhard. *Das Buch Jesaia.* 3d ed. Göttingen: Vandenhoeck & Ruprecht, 1914.

Duty, Guy. *Escape from the Coming Tribulation: How to Be Prepared for the Last Great Crisis of History.* Minneapolis: Bethany Fellowship, 1975.

Edwards, Richard Alan. *The Sign of Jonah: In the Theology of the Evangelists and Q.* Alec R. Allenson, 1971.

Festinger, Leon, *et al. When Prophecy Fails.* University of Minnesota Press, 1956.

Gilkey, Langdon. *Reaping the Whirlwind: A Christian Interpretation of History.* Seabury Press, 1976.

Glassman, Carl. "And They Shall Take Up Serpents." *Des Moines Sunday Register,* April 2, 1978.

Graham, Billy. *World Aflame.* Minneapolis: The Billy Graham Evangelistic Association, 1965.

Hamilton, Michael P., ed. *The Charismatic Movement.* Wm. B. Eerdmans Publishing Co., 1975.

Hanson, Richard S. *The Future of the Late Great Planet Earth: What Does Biblical Prophecy Mean for You?* Augsburg Publishing House, 1972

Hengel, Martin. *Nachfolge und Charisma: Eine exegetisch-religionsgeschichtliche Studie zu Mt 8:21f. und Jesu Ruf in die Nachfolge.* Berlin: Töpelmann, 1968.

———. *Victory Over Violence.* Tr. by D. E. Green. Fortress Press, 1973.

——. *Die Zeloten: Untersuchungen zur jüdischen Freiheitsbewegung in der Zeit von Herodes I bis 70 n. Chr.* Leiden: E. J. Brill, 1961.

Hersey, John Richard. *Hiroshima.* Alfred A. Knopf, 1946.

Jeremias, Joachim. *The Central Message of the New Testament.* Charles Scribner's Sons, 1965.

——. *The Eucharistic Words of Jesus.* Tr. by Norman Perrin. Charles Scribner's Sons, 1966.

——. *Jesus' Promise to the Nations.* Tr. by S. H. Hooke. Alec R. Allenson, 1958.

——. *New Testament Theology: The Proclamation of Jesus.* Tr. by John Bowden. Charles Scribner's Sons, 1971.

Jewett, Robert. *The Captain America Complex: The Dilemma of Zealous Nationalism.* Westminster Press, 1973.

——, and Lawrence, John Shelton. *The American Monomyth.* Doubleday & Company, Anchor Books, 1977.

Johnson, Paul. *History of Christianity.* London: Weidenfeld & Nicolson, 1976.

Jorstad, Erling, ed. *The Holy Spirit in Today's Church: A Handbook of the New Pentecostalism.* Abingdon Press, 1973.

Kelber, Werner. *The Kingdom in Mark: A New Place and a New Time.* Fortress Press, 1974.

Lindsey, Hal. *There's a New World Coming.* Fleming H. Revell Company, Spire Christian Comics, 1974

Lindsey, Hal, and Carlson, C. C. *The Late Great Planet Earth.* Zondervan Publishing House, 1970.

——. *The Liberation of Planet Earth.* Zondervan Publishing House, 1974.

——. *Satan Is Alive and Well on Planet Earth.* Zondervan Publishing House, 1972.

——. *The Terminal Generation.* Fleming H. Revell Company, 1976.

Lockyer, Herbert. *All the Messianic Prophecies of the Bible.* Zondervan Publishing House, 1973.

——. *The Rapture of Saints.* London: Pickering & Inglis, 1938.

MacArthur, Harry H., *et al. The Rapture: Our Lord's Coming for His Church.* American Prophetic League, 1940.

Marsh, Spencer. *God, Man and Archie Bunker.* Harper & Row, Publishers, 1975.

Müller, Ulrich B. "Vision und Botschaft: Erwägungen zur prophetischen Struktur der Verkündigung Jesu." *Zeitschrift für Theologie und Kirche.* Vol. LXXIV, 1974, pp. 416–448.

Nunn, Clyde Z. "The Rising Credibility of the Devil in America." *Listening: Journal of Religion and Culture,* Vol. IX, 1974, pp. 84–100.

———. *Tolerance for Non-Conformity.* Jossey-Bass, 1978.

O'Connor, Flannery. "Everything That Rises Must Converge," and "Revelation," from *Everything That Rises Must Converge,* by Flannery O'Connor. Farrar, Straus & Giroux, 1965.

———. "A Good Man Is Hard to Find," from *A Good Man Is Hard to Find,* by Flannery O'Connor. Harcourt, Brace & Company, 1955.

Ogden, Schubert M. *The Reality of God and Other Essays.* Harper & Row, Publishers, 1963.

Pentecost, J. Dwight. *Prophecy for Today: The Middle East Crisis and the Future of the World.* Zondervan Publishing House, 1961.

———. *Things to Come: A Study in Biblical Eschatology.* 1958. Zondervan Publishing House, 1974.

———. *Will Man Survive? Prophecy You Can Understand.* Moody Press, 1972.

Percy, Walker. *Lancelot: A Novel.* Farrar, Straus & Giroux, 1977.

Perrin, Norman. *Rediscovering the Teachings of Jesus.* Harper & Row, Publishers, 1967.

Potok, Chaim. *The Chosen: A Novel.* Simon & Schuster, 1967.

Pranger, Robert J. "Nuclear War Comes to the Mideast." *Worldview,* Vol. XX, July-August, 1977.

Rhoads, David M. *Israel in Revolution: 6–74 C.E. A Political History Based on the Writings of Josephus.* Fortress Press, 1976.

Robinson, James M. *The Problem of History in Mark.* Alec R. Allenson, 1957.

Safrai, S. "The Temple." In M. De Jonge *et al.* (eds.), *The Jewish People in the First Century,* Vol. II. Fortress Press, 1976.

Sandeen, Ernest R. *The Roots of Fundamentalism.* University of Chicago Press, 1970.

Sanders, James A. "From Isaiah 61 to Luke 4," in Jacob Neusner (ed.), *Christianity, Judaism and Other Greco-Roman Cults: Studies for Morton Smith at Sixty.* Leiden: E. J. Brill, 1975. Vol. I, pp. 75–106.

Simbro, William. "Christian Business Directory Chief: God Is Narrow-Minded." *Des Moines Sunday Register,* Jan. 29, 1978.

Smith, Wilbur M. *You Can Know the Future.* Glendale, Calif.: Regal Books, 1971.

Stedman, Ray C. *What on Earth's Going to Happen?* Glendale, Calif.: Regal Books, 1970.

Stott, John R. W. *The Authority of the Bible.* Inter-Varsity Press, 1974.

Strauss, Lehman. *God's Plan for the Future.* Zondervan Publishing House, 1975.

Sumrall, Ken. *What's Your Question?* Springdale, Pa.: Whitaker House, 1972.

Towner, W. Sibley. *How God Deals with Evil.* Westminster Press, 1976.

Walvoord, John F., and Walvoord, John E. *Armageddon: Oil and the Middle East Crisis.* Zondervan Publishing House, 1976. Rev. ed.

White, John Wesley. *WW III: Signs of the Impending Battle of Armageddon.* Zondervan Publishing House, 1977.

Wilburn, Gary. "The Doomsday Chic." *Christianity Today,* Jan. 27, 1978, pp. 22–23.

Wilkerson, David. *Racing Toward Judgment.* Fleming H. Revell Company, 1976.

———. *The Vision.* Fleming H. Revell Company, 1974.

Wilson, Dwight. *Armageddon Now! The Premillenarian Response to Russia and Israel Since 1917.* Baker Book House, 1977.

Wood, Leon J. *The Bible & Future Events: An Introductory Survey of Last-Day Events.* Zondervan Publishing House, 1973.

Woodward, Kenneth L.; Gram, Dewey; and Lisle, Laurie. "The Boom in Doom." *Newsweek,* Jan. 10, 1977, pp. 41–51.

———, and Mark, Rachel. "Christians for Israel." *Newsweek,* Nov. 28, 1977, p. 126.

Yadin, Yigael. *Bar-Kokhba: The Rediscovery of the Legendary Hero of the Second Jewish Revolt Against Rome.* Random House, Inc., 1971.

———. *Masada: Herod's Fortress and the Zealots' Last Stand.* Tr. by Moshe Pearlman. Random House, 1966.